HOW TO REMODEL A MAN

ALSO BY W. BRUCE CAMERON

8 Simple Rules for Dating My Teenage Daughter:
And Other Tips from a Beleagured Father
(Not That Any of Them Work)

HOW TO REMODEL A MAN

Tips and Techniques on
Accomplishing Something
You Know Is Impossible
but Want to Try Anyway

W. BRUCE CAMERON

ST. MARTIN'S PRESS

New York

www.stmartins.com

BOOK DESIGN BY AMANDA DEWEY

Library of Congress Cataloging-in-Publication Data

Cameron, W. Bruce.
How to remodel a man : tips and techniques on accomplishing something you know is impossible but want to try anyway / W. Bruce Cameron.—1st ed.
    p. cm.
ISBN 0-312-33317-X
EAN 978-0312-33317-1
    1. Men—Humor. I. Title.

PN6231.M45C26   2004
814'.6—dc22

                                        2004046786

First Edition: September 2004

10 9 8 7 6 5 4 3 2 1

This book is dedicated to my father,

WILLIAM J. CAMERON, M.D.,

the original unremodeled man.

CONTENTS

ACKNOWLEDGMENTS

First and foremost I must thank all the readers of my column, both on the Internet and in the newspapers, for being so intelligent and discerning and for responding so enthusiastically, even sort of frighteningly, to the idea that I was compiling a list of male faults because I didn't have any myself. Then I have to thank John Temple and Maria Cote at the *Rocky Mountain News* for printing my column even when, in their judgment, they might have been better off publishing a big blank space. Thanks to Mary Winter, my first editor at the *Rocky*, who was so overwhelmed by what she had done that she took early retirement. Thanks to all the other editors who publish my column in their newspapers, and thanks to Al Gore for inventing the Internet so that before I was in the papers I had a place where I could publish myself.

My new home at St. Martin's could not be more wonderful and

it has everything to do with Diane Reverand, a positive, professional, and caring editor who truly wants nothing more or less than for her writers to follow their dreams. Thanks to Regina Scarpa for all of her help, like forcing Diane to read her e-mails.

Thanks to everyone who bought my book *8 Simple Rules for Dating My Teenage Daughter* and who watches the show on ABC. If nobody had read *8 Simple Rules* I doubt anybody would have wanted to publish this one. Thanks to ABC for keeping the show on the air through everything, and to John Ritter, loved by everyone, taken from us all way too soon.

Thanks to Jody Rein for discovering me when I was an unpublished writer and for being there for me during the sale of this book and every wretched clause and sub clause of the contract. Thanks Johnna Hietala for discovering Jody Rein and for helping with all the paperwork.

Thanks to Ted and Evie Michon for lending me their genius.

Thanks to Maria Hjelm for her intelligent editorial notes and for having a last name that causes me to clear my throat.

Thanks to my children for letting me write about them, or at least for not being able to think of any effective way to prevent it.

Thanks to Gary Loder, Heather Colcord, and Todd Christopher for their expert bullfighting. Gary, having you on my side means the world to me. Thanks to Alex Hertzberg, Danny Sherman, and Terry Norton-Wright for giving me a blueprint to follow for my future.

Thanks to my friend George Bloom for telling me I dress so poorly.

Thanks to my mom for trying to remodel my dad, and to my dad for resisting it so totally.

Thanks to Lisa Craig, my Web master, for turning www.wbruce cameron.com into the best Web site in the entire universe for attracting discriminating humor readers; if you don't believe me, just go there and look. Thanks to Bill Finch for helping with artistic concepts, and to Paul Dalen for creating the original Web site.

Thanks to Marcia Wallace for not looking back, and to Norma Vela for having a teen party for me and for introducing me to Gary, and to Julie Cypher for producing a baby at the right moment, and to Jen Watson for finding me a girlfriend.

Thanks to Diane Driscoll for inviting me to all the parties that are past my curfew.

Thanks to Rhona Raskin for wanting to talk to me in Seattle and for where the conversation went.

I want to acknowledge the National Society of Newspaper Columnists for selecting me as the best humor columnist and thank all of my friends there.

Thanks to Leah Gonzales for being on the ball these past two years.

Thanks to Marcia Wallace (again), Mary McCormack, and Ileen Getz for showing up with me to support me as my celebrity babes for the taping of the *8 Simple Rules* pilot.

Thanks to Oliver North for all of his help with my career.

Thanks to Creators Syndicate for making my column available to people all over the world.

Thanks to John Walsh for making me one of America's most wanted authors, and to Wayne Brady for having me on his fantastic show (which should still be on the air!).

Thanks to Bob Bridges for his volunteer work in proofreading my columns so that my newspaper thinks I can write professionally.

If you expected to see your name here and don't, it is probably because I didn't think you'd want me to call your name out publicly. It is not because I forgot you. Thanks to you for everything you did; I am very grateful.

Finally, thanks to Cathryn Michon, for all of her encouragement and notes and support through the writing of *How to Remodel a*

Man, and to Coors Brewing Company for its help with inspiration, and to whoever owns those yappy dogs next door for making sure I got up in the morning to write. Okay, reading this, I realize that it makes Cathryn look about as important to me as a can of beer, and even if we're talking about lots of cans of beers, that's still not enough. Cathryn is the single most inspiring person in my life. She holds me to the highest standards and gives me the courage to do the same for myself. Thank you, Cathryn.

PREFACE

Why I Wrote This Book

I am a Changed Man.

I declare these words proudly, as a testament to the triumph of human will over a seemingly indomitable challenge: my gender. You see, I was born a man—well actually, I was born a baby (same thing, some people might say), but I was a *male* baby—and change does not come easily to a male, because they just don't see why they should bother. Attempting to modify a man's behavior is like trying to talk cats into playing the tuba—even if you can convince them to put their lips on the thing, they'll never understand *why*. Yet there are people out there in the world endeavoring every single day to do the seemingly impossible: change men.

For want of a better term, I'll call these people "women."

Now, I'm not a woman, nor do I have any plans to become one. It's too expensive, and the shoes look really uncomfortable. But I am the first male person of my gender to alter his very nature in an effort to become a better man. Along the way, I derived some methods that can be used on less enlightened males to remodel *their* behavior—and these methods are contained in this book.

You might wonder why it is that I would betray my gender—for which I have developed a certain fondness—and reveal to all the women in the world in easy, step-by-step instructions, how to re-model a man. Is it for riches, for fame, for the unrestrained adora-tion of every single female on the face of the planet?

Actually, if I thought I'd get any of that, I would have done this years ago. No, my decision to join forces with people of a sex dif-ferent than mine is based on my simple observation that men have been running things around here for a long time now, and as far as I can see, we're not doing all that great a job. I think that if women were in charge, there would be fewer bank robberies and bar fights and movie titles containing the words "bikini car wash."

Of course, it will be a long time before women are allowed to run the planet. Men generally don't vote for women to hold high government offices, believing that females aren't quite ready to handle the most important responsibility that comes with such au-thority: which is to let men continue to be in charge. So until that day arrives, the best we can hope to do is to modify the behavior of men.

To start with, I had to focus on what it is about men that needs to be changed. I'm no sociologist, but, as an author, I do spend a lot of time studying men, learning their various habits and man-ners and even living among them. I've been to their houses and eaten their "man food," all in the name of learning more about these strange creatures who have become such a fixture of modern life. Yet when I met my buddies at the sports bar to talk about our flaws, none of us could think of anything that needed to be changed!

The best we could come up with is that often men become so

dedicated to completing their mission they lose sight of everything else. We're linear and focused; once we get started on a job, it's hard for us to stop until we're done. Then the hockey game came on, and we sort of lost interest in the topic.

I thought about asking the women in my life—my daughters, my sisters, even my mother—but the first response I got, "Men are always taking credit for stuff that women come up with," demonstrated to me just how unpleasant that method would be.

Then I came up with a brilliant idea. The inspiration for it came from my daughter, who said, "Why don't you set up a place on your Web site for women to write in and tell you what it is about men they would like to see changed?" My idea was this: I would set up a place on my Web site for women to write in and tell me what it is about men they would like to see changed!

I reasoned that even if I only received half a dozen ideas, it would be a big help. I put up the form on my Web site (www.wbrucecameron.com) and sat back, hoping I would eventually hear from somebody.

I received more than three thousand entries in the first month.

Reading through the e-mails, many of which were very alarming because they seemed to be complaints about some of *my* most adorable traits, I concluded that men are in big trouble. We haven't been listening (one of the most frequent criticisms) to what women are saying, and let me tell you, some of these women are mad.

I view *How to Remodel a Man* as the story of one man's journey to Changed Man, but along the way I took into consideration the common gripes sent to me by females all over the planet. Some of the grievances—like the woman who says her boyfriend thinks it's funny to drop his pants and show his butt to people, including her parents—I wasn't able to help with. Others, like men who won't ask for directions or men who can't put their dirty socks in the clothes hamper, but can put them *on top* of the hamper, I am able to provide clear directions on how to remodel. In the process, I've painted a fairly unflattering portrait of the male of the species— but I don't think I'm telling anyone what they didn't already know.

Am I worried that men will pick up this book, see that I've provided instructions on how to remodel a man, and want to kill me?

Of course not.

Men don't read instructions.

1.

- -- -

RESISTANCE TO CHANGE

Men Just Figure It Would Be Easier
If *You* Changed Instead

Women are willing to purchase a man off the rack, but then they want to take him home and make alterations. They'll witness some adorable trait—such as a man's inability to stand before an open refrigerator and locate the jar of mayonnaise within it—and want to fix it.

Men don't want to be "fixed." Men want women to love them just the way they are. Men don't want to adopt such unnatural traits as sensitivity or thoughtfulness. And when I say men want women "to love them," I mean, of course, "to have sex with them."

Unfortunately, men don't really understand why women would want to have sex with them. *We* sure wouldn't want to! It must be, we conclude, because we are so manly. And what are manly traits? How about strength and resolve? To have strength and resolve means to be unyielding and uncompromising. So men will be unyielding and uncompromising in their belief that they shouldn't have to go grocery shopping, and somehow conclude that this makes them more desirable to women!

Yet paradoxically I wouldn't be a Changed Man today if it weren't for the feeling that I needed to adopt a new strategy when it came to attracting members of the female sex. After my divorce, I went through a long period of time when I didn't feel like dating anyone, followed by an even longer period when it seemed no one really felt like dating me. I'd ask a woman out, and it would go very well—we'd get to know each other over dinner, with me relating my likes and dislikes, telling her where I stood on critical issues of the day such as the Instant Replay Rule in football. I'd considerately steer the conversation back on track whenever my date brought up a topic I didn't think she'd find interesting, like her job or her friends—stuff she already knew about and was probably sick of discussing. My dates all seemed fascinated with me—by the end of the evening, most of them were so spellbound by my narrative they quit talking and just nodded appreciatively. Yet when I called these same women for a second date, they all demurred, using excuses like, "I can't on Saturday, I'm joining the Witness Protection Program" or "I've come to realize I am a man trapped in a woman's body."

When my ex-wife got remarried, I was happy for her, but it spotlighted my own dismal situation. Though I had gotten used to living on my own, I missed the sort of connection one gets from a long-term relationship with a female of the opposite sex, not just the physical part, but all of it. I plunged into a depressive, self-loathing state—and immediately got on the phone so that friends and relatives could assure me that there was nothing wrong with me at all.

You can't get enough of this sort of objective feedback, so one of the people I called was my sister, who didn't seem to understand the moral support that was expected of her.

"The way you're headed, you'll be single for the rest of your life," she suggested cheerfully.

I should explain that I have two sisters: a doctor sister, who thinks she is smarter than I am, and a teacher sister, who thinks the same thing. Both are younger and both are wrong. In this case, I was talking to my doctor sister, but it could have been the teacher; they're interchangeable, in my view.

"But all and all, women find me very attractive," I prompted, letting her know what she was supposed to be saying.

"Your experience suggests otherwise."

"Well, what's wrong with these women, then, that they don't want to go out with me more than once?"

"The problem," my sister said in a fake I'm-a-doctor-so-let-me-diagnose-the-illness tone, "is that you have a lot of character flaws and you aren't willing to change."

"Flaws?" I sputtered. "What are you talking about? What flaws?"

"You want me to name them all?" she asked incredulously.

"I sure hope you never talk to your patients like this," I told her.

We hung up and I thought about what she had said. She had known me my whole life. She'd seen me grow up in a house mostly filled with women and had watched me experience a marriage and daughters and a woman boss and even a female physician.

From my unchanged man point of view, was it any wonder I had flaws? All my life I'd been surrounded by women!

I felt much better and was willing to let the matter go, now that I understood it. This is a typically male approach to problem solving: All we really care about is determining who is to blame. Then I thought about my social calendar, which was strikingly bereft of any female company. I called my sister back.

"Well, okay," I told her. "What if I admitted that I had some of these semi-flawlike characteristics, and might be willing to . . ." I swallowed hard. "To change them a little. Nothing major! But if I did, what would you say are these so-called failings?"

Now, I don't know what I had in mind when I came up with this, though I am pretty sure whatever it was fell into the category of

"Not Much." But my sister, who you'd think would have enough to do already, decided to take it upon herself to compile a list for me. Without my permission, she began inviting other women from my life to join her in the project. Soon the ranks were swelling, including my other sister, my mother, my daughters, and even my junior high school counselor!

I shouldn't have been surprised that she was able to find so many females willing to subscribe to the absurd premise that I needed some sort of group effort dedicated to fixing me. I believe women are often very enthusiastic about forming committees, particularly if they can have meetings and eat chocolate. Men, on the other hand, prefer to form teams: highly integrated, collaborative groups that get together and argue about who gets to be in charge.

"We've decided you don't just need to be changed, you need to be totally remodeled," she chirped. "Sort of like, *This Old House,* only in this case it's, 'This Old Man.' Get it?"

"Totally remodeled? I thought you were just going to give me a list of my supposed faults and send them to me so I could see which ones I disagreed with."

"Well . . . why don't you make your list, and I'll make mine, and then we'll compare?"

This suggestion contained an element I found very distasteful: personal effort. But I saw her point—who knew my minor imperfections better than I? I worked on it for a while, and here's what I came up with:

W. BRUCE CAMERON'S LIST OF SUPPOSED FAULTS

1. Often times I'll sit down to make a list of things I need to get done, but I never seem to do anything on the list. Obviously, I need to learn how to delegate.
2. I really need a sports car of some kind.

3. Usually when a woman is telling me her problems, I will interrupt her and give her advice on how to fix them. I think what women really want is not for me to jump in with solutions, but for me to wait until they are finished talking before I tell them what to do.

4. I can't afford to run out and buy every shiny new gadget that comes on the market. I need to make more money so that I can.

"I made your list," I told my sister. "It's a little long."

"We came up with a hundred and seventy-eight," she replied, "but we haven't heard from Mom yet. Also Mrs. Bunting said she has some."

Mrs. Bunting lived across the street from us when I was in the fourth grade.

"What? A hundred and seventy-eight? You're supposed to be counting my faults, not my, my . . ."

"Remaining hair follicles?" my sister suggested innocently.

"I think it's a little excessive to run up the score like this."

"I forgot that one: 'Always uses sports analogies.' "

"Would you cut it out? You are turning this into way too big a deal."

Feeling that she had lost all perspective and was behaving in a fashion so irrational she might wind up losing her license to practice medicine, I decided to turn to an impartial third person—my friend and coworker Sarah—who I knew would be on my side.

Sarah works in the lifestyle department at the newspaper where I am a columnist. She's a couple of years younger than I, and I would probably consider her attractive if it were not for the squat, ugly wedge of a boyfriend she lives with, an unpleasant, thick-skulled guy named Doug. I've pledged to Sarah I'll keep an open mind about him, but he's a real jerk.

I apparently failed to explain the situation adequately, because

Sarah immediately became excited about the whole process. "Tell your sister I'm in!" she enthused.

"What? There's nothing to be 'in.' What's happening is that my sister has gone overboard and you agree with that."

"What would be so bad about changing your behavior a little? Maybe if you addressed your failings, it would be easier to find someone to love you."

I pondered this. "When you say, 'to love,' do you mean what I think you mean?"

"I think I've told you before, it wouldn't hurt for you to be a little more communicative," she reminded me.

"Ah." I waved my hand.

"And what does that mean?" she asked impatiently.

"Just, you know, I'm already communicative."

"Or more sensitive," Sarah plunged on. "Remember when you told Maria she had an 'old baby'?"

"What? It's just that Mallory had a newborn, a fresh baby. So Maria's baby wasn't the number one new baby anymore. I can't help that," I protested. "But hey, didn't I go to a movie with you that was French?"

"You complained the whole time! People kept telling you to shush!"

"Which just goes to show how idiotic it was," I argued smugly. "Why did they need me to be quiet? It was in French. What, I was interrupting the subtitles?"

"And that's your idea of being sensitive," she stated flatly. "To tell Maria her baby is somehow past its expiration date, and to sit there in a French movie and speculate on how long it has been since the lead actress has had a bath."

I thought about this. "Well, maybe you've got a point."

"Breakthrough!" she exulted. "So are you saying you want to be more sensitive? You want to be more in touch with your feelings?" Her voice softened. "Hey Bruce, are you really saying you want to be a Changed Man? Because if you are, I'm your friend, I can help."

This made me pause. Sarah was touching on something deep and personal here, inviting me to open up about my feelings of loneliness and frustration, offering me an intimate confidence that men rarely experience. I cleared my throat. "How do you think the Broncos are going to do this year?"

"What? Why would you ask something like that?"

"Well, because of the quarterback situation, duh," I responded logically.

"I thought we were talking about making profound changes in the way you do things, to be less self-centered and more considerate," she countered.

"Wouldn't it be easier just to give me a list of women who would like 'to love' me?"

"You know why you won't change? Because you don't have to. A man can behave any way he wants, and women are expected to accommodate it."

"Sounds like one of those if-it-ain't-broke-don't-fix-it situations," I agreed.

"It all started when women decided to let men be the hunters," she fumed. "Men went out to look for something to throw a spear at, and when they couldn't find anything, they started throwing spears at each other. Then it was about who had the biggest spear, then later, the biggest gun, the biggest missiles . . . of course, we both know what we're really talking about, here."

"In high school I was called Bruce 'The Cannon' Cameron. Just saying," I interjected.

"If you really remodeled yourself, and wrote about it, women everywhere would thank you."

"I'll pass, thanks anyway."

"Most women feel like they have to use psychological tricks to get a man to change," my friend continued. "But that wouldn't work with you. You're incapable of change."

"Not incapable, just not motivated," I corrected, feeling a little insulted.

"No, it would be too difficult. Impossible," she insisted.

"Actually, no, that's not the issue. I could do it if I wanted."

"No, you can't."

"Yes I can!"

"You're afraid," she sniffed.

"What? That's ridiculous." Now I was mad.

"Then prove it."

"Fine!"

Feeling under siege from everyone—my sister, Sarah, even Mrs. Bunting—I decided to give this Changed Man thing a try, if only to prove that I wasn't afraid, which I think we can all agree is a really ridiculous idea. Your man, however, may not be as open-minded as I am. To break down his resistance to change, you may have to employ the sneaky psychological tricks to which Sarah was referring.

Obviously, I'm not perfect. I started with (a lot fewer than 178) faults. But I have changed, and I honestly feel that I am a better man for it. What you'll learn from my story is that often changing a man is a matter of using certain techniques to make him feel that it is all his idea. Ask him point-blank to alter his behavior, and he'll turn you down. Apply a more subtle strategy, and you, too, can remodel your man.

Let's get started!

Simple Test to See If Someone Should Be Remodeled

Question 1: Is he a man? Yes

No

(continued)

Simple Test to See If Someone
Should Be Remodeled (continued)

Scoring: Give one point for every "Yes" answer.

Score: 0 = No remodeling necessary.
1 = Definitely needs remodeling.

THIS WON'T BE EASY

When males are first born, they are pretty simple to change: You just grab them by the ankles, lift, and pull off their diapers. (For a lot of men, gripping them in the pants is still the best way to capture their attention.) As they get older, they become more set in their ways. Ask a man to alter an aspect of his behavior and he'll most likely conclude there is something wrong with *you*.

A clear illustration of this male attitude toward women who would change men is offered by the story of Adam and Eve. As men tell it, there was Adam, pretty happy in the Garden of Eden. His meals were provided as part of his rent, he probably took a lot of naps. Then what happens? Eve comes along and asks Adam to change. And with that, humans are kicked out of the garden and forced to commute to work. Moral of the story: Eve should have just kept quiet and let Adam be the way he was.

You can see why men keep telling this story over and over; it proves that if you try to remodel a man, you're going to get God really mad at you. This is an example of male logic, which is the process of making up your mind and then looking for facts to support your conclusion.

What men always seem to ignore is that until Eve arrived, Adam didn't even have his own apartment. He'd never tasted beer, and there was no place to get a decent hamburger. He slept in the dirt, and was so oblivious he didn't even realize he was naked. Even worse, he didn't seem to notice that Eve was naked, either.

That's just how men are: They don't seem to pay much attention to their surroundings. It takes a woman to point out that living conditions could be improved a little. For example, my cousin just bought a big screen television for his tiny apartment. The thing is so huge it blocks access to the bathroom. To get to the toilet, you have to squeeze through a narrow gap about six inches wide, which nobody bothers to do because his place is so close to the alley. His fiancée refuses to spend the night there, and one of these days it will dawn on my cousin why. Like Adam, he'll suddenly realize that if he ever wants to see a naked woman in his garden, he'll have to find a nicer place to live.

So yes, my cousin will be a Changed Man, at least when it comes to this one area. But it is wearing to suppose that every time you want your man to do something, you have to show him your, um, forbidden fruit. That's why this book is so valuable: There are other tactics you can use that don't always involve nudity.

It's not easy. In fact, it is very similar to what happens when you set out to remodel a house—though most people who have taken on the task of building an addition vow never to do it again, while most people who have attempted to change a man usually keep trying. Both processes are equally frustrating, though houses won't actively fight remodeling the way men do.

But that doesn't mean men can't change. I didn't want to change, either.

So if you think you're up to the challenge, the first step in remodeling your man is to tear down what's already in place. And to do that, you have to understand how he was raised.

2.

- - -

LORD OF THE MANOR

Men Doing Housework—
Not as Rare as a Solar Eclipse,
but About as Useful

W hen I was a little boy, I had it made. My parents organized family chores to emulate what they saw on black-and-white television: men swaggered around doing manly things, like building barns and digging wells, and the women handled the housework, waltzing through the living room with the vacuum cleaner as if dancing with Fred Astaire. Since our water poured freely from the city water system and building a barn would have violated local zoning laws, my father and I were Lords of the Manor, and my mom and two younger sisters were Cinderellas.

I thought it was a really good system.

Did I notice that it was patently unfair and that my sisters were putting in far more hours doing so-called women's work than I was devoting to men's work? You betcha. I could hardly not notice it, as my sisters complained about it every night. I was learning one of life's great lessons for males: women may work harder than men, but men should never acknowledge this fact.

It's no accident surveys show men claim to do their fair share of housework, even if the only real housework they've done in the past week is to fill out the survey. I was able to ignore my sisters' complaints because I was convinced that men's work is just, well, harder. Not that I was actually doing any. I suppose I saw myself on standby, like those pilots who were ready to race out to their planes whenever a Soviet blip threatened American airspace.

This is why a man can watch TV with a woman and not make a move to help her fold laundry during the show: In a man's world, everyone has an assigned task. His task is to shovel the snow out of the driveway. Your task is to fold laundry. See how well the system works? Shoveling snow is a hard job! Would it be fair for him to fold laundry and shovel snow? No way! Does the fact that it's July have any bearing on the matter? Why should it? What counts is when it snows, he'll be out there in the thick of it, working like a man! Unless he strains his back, and then he might need you to do it.

So I was more than a little outraged when my mother announced one evening that from that point forward, I would be part of the kitchen duty roster, rotating in as if I were one of the girls. Where was the justice in this edict, handed down after a secret trial in which I had no testimony? I turned a disbelieving glance at my key ally, my father, but his cowardly eyes wouldn't meet mine. The system that had kept his own hands free from dish soap was under assault, and he was maintaining a low profile to avoid being caught in the dragnet of the new regime.

After dinner, my sisters bolted. I watched them from the window as they played in the backyard, seething at their selfishness. Weren't we a family? Weren't we supposed to all help each other?

Well, okay. I turned my attention back to the dishes. They were a mess, a disaster. It was hopeless.

"I can't do it," I told my mother, who was working at her desk. "There are all these dirty pans."

"It will be easy once you get started," she answered in a voice that sounded kind but in fact was pure evil. "Scrub the pans. Put the leftovers in the refrigerator."

"Scrub the pans?"

"You can do it, Bruce," she encouraged me. Her faith in me was so absolute I could only conclude that I had the worst mother in the world.

I jammed my hands into my pockets and sullenly returned to the kitchen. My sisters were pulling ice cream sandwiches from the freezer. "Hey!" I shouted. I went to find my mom. "It's no fair, my sisters are making even more of a mess, and I was almost done!"

"Don't forget to wipe down the counters," she replied in a mind-boggling change of subject.

Wipe the counters? Since when were the counters part of cleaning the kitchen? Was life even worth living anymore?

I stood and gazed with pain-filled eyes at the table, still laden with the remains of the night's dinner. Why did people even bother to make meals if it was going to cause such a problem afterward? Why couldn't we just eat ice cream bars from the freezer?

"I think I've got a fever," I told my mom.

"As soon as you're done with the dishes, you should go lie down," she replied.

I went back and picked up a pan, sniffing at the dried-out spaghetti sauce.

"The stuff's all stuck to the pans," I announced, back in my mother's den. "I'll have to throw them away."

"Soak the pans first, then scrub them."

Well, I'd been doing dishes for nearly half an hour, with no appreciable progress. I listlessly went to the freezer for an ice cream bar.

"I don't hear any work going on in there!" my mother called with psychotic cheerfulness.

Well, maybe that's because my head was chopped off by the Russian army! I seethed back silently. *Maybe because I'm doing dishes, which is not my job, the Russians were able to sneak in here and kill me and eat all our ice cream bars and you don't even know because you are a Terrible Mother.*

"Bruce?"

Fine, you want noise? I turned on the garbage disposal, filling the house with a hungry roar as it sucked down the water in the sink in a violent swirl. *There, happy, Mom? I'm doing the dishes while America loses the Cold War!*

The disposal kept churning. It was the mouth of Glork, I decided, who came from the planet Quork and lived under the sink. His ravenous appetite must be sated or he would pull down the entire house in his vortex. I began scraping plates into his black maw.

I must have more, Glork roared.

No time to put the leftovers into the refrigerator, I poured them straight down Glork's throat. For a moment, he seemed satisfied, and then he bellowed in rage. We'd had fish the night before. I found some wrapped in foil and into Glork's mouth it went. Eggs were vaporized in seconds, though a head of lettuce kept Glork grinding happily for more than a minute. Carrots and cheese and pickles, but still Glork screamed, and I could feel the gravitational forces shifting, spinning me helplessly through the kitchen. I clutched a chair, but it served as no impediment as Glork dragged me toward the center of the maelstrom. Frantic, I gathered a handful of silverware and tossed it into Glork's terrible teeth.

This drew the attention of my father. He arrived just in time for Glork's clanking, thrashing death, and in the sudden stillness that followed, asked me what I was doing.

"Cleaning the kitchen," I responded obviously. I thought my father, a man himself, would be impressed by how ably I had demonstrated what dire consequences might follow when males were entrusted with this sort of work, but he seemed fixated on why I had jammed a bunch of forks into Glork's mouth, which I thought sort of missed the larger point.

What I was really doing was working a scam that men try all the time: attempting to prove they shouldn't be involved in housework by deliberately failing at the assigned task.*

Here's an example: You send a man into a grocery store with a list of items. An hour later he returns to the car with only half the things you asked for, plus a vat of barbecue flavored cheese balls because a pretty woman was handing out samples on aisle six. Even worse, he couldn't find the tofu, so he bought what he figured was a reasonable substitute—vanilla pudding—handing it to you without a trace of guile on his face.

Obviously, he could have located the tofu if he had just asked someone, but it is a lot easier to just grab some pudding, circle around for another cheese ball, and then head out to the parking lot and declare himself unworthy of ever again being assigned such an important job.

If this ever happens to you, you'll be tempted to have this conversation:

YOU:

What were you thinking? I can't use pudding.

HIM:

Why not? Isn't it practically the same thing?

Of course it is not. Pudding is dessert. Tofu is a gelatinous mass of white gunk that tastes like wet cement. Men know this, otherwise, they would *eat* tofu.

---

*If my father had been a good parent, he would have chided me for such an obvious scam and would have taught me that men need to be much more subtle. Instead, he just made me do the dishes. With this kind of upbringing, it is a wonder I didn't wind up as some kind of criminal!

YOU:

It's not the same! Obviously I can never send you shopping again.

HIM:

Oh darn!

TIP › Can you see that by being focused on the short-term goal of preparing an inedible meal, you've lost sight of the larger strategy of teaching your man to shop for groceries? Here's the conversation you should have had when he returned to the car, all proud of himself.

YOU:

I see that you bought vanilla pudding instead of tofu.

HIM:

Yeah, I figured it is practically the same thing.

YOU:

What a smart idea! Actually, though, I need tofu because I'm planning to lay some bricks with the leftovers. So go back and find the tofu.

HIM:

I guess I'll go back, then. Tofu? Would that be in the same section as milk of magnesia, maybe?

YOU:

I'm sure you'll find it in due course without asking anyone.

If you use this tactic, he will eventually emerge from the store, triumphantly carrying a package of the loathsome tofu, which he will present to you as if he had killed it with his own hands. "Oh honey," you should gush, "you're wonderful! You did a great job!"

"I did?" He'll frown, suddenly realizing that in his excitement over stalking and killing the tofu, he sort of blew the gaff, as con men say. But you've got him trapped, now; if he can track down tofu, he can find anything, and he'll have to do the grocery shopping from that point forward until he thinks of a different ruse.

THE SCAM IN ACTION: MEN AREN'T EVEN VERY CLEVER AT BEING CLEVER

I have a friend named Marv who is an airplane mechanic. All day long he works with intricate machines. His wife is a manager of something manageable in the banking industry, and she washes the dishes every night because, in her words, "Marvin just can't wash dishes. He's terrible at it."

Here's how I feel about that: If I ever look out the window and see Marv working on my jet engine, I'm getting off the plane. What sort of man toils with hydraulics all day and then claims he can't slide a wet plate into the correct slot in a dishwasher?

Or take Dr. Richards, a surgeon acquaintance of mine. He has never helped his wife in the kitchen, even though she runs her own business and hasn't taken a vacation since the last moon mission. His excuse: If the knife slipped and he accidentally sliced his hands, he wouldn't be able to make a living. "What if I cut my tendon?" he demands, because as a surgeon he knows how hard it is to fix something like that.

I can't explain why Marv's wife appears to fall for the aircraft-mechanic-who-can't-wash-dishes routine, though I will note that every time they go on a vacation, she insists on taking the train. But a surgeon who is unable to use a knife? If I were Mrs. Richards, I'd announce loudly at a party, "My husband? He can't even slice a tomato without the knife getting away from him!"

That would certainly silence anyone in the room scheduled for a vasectomy.

Men cheerfully admit domestic incompetence in social groups only as long as it contributes to their standing among other men. When a woman says, "My husband Phil is terrible at vacuuming. It's easier for me to just do it!"

PHIL THINKS:

I'm adorable!

THE MEN IN THE ROOM THINK:

Whoa, Phil, great scam you've got going there!

THE WOMEN IN THE ROOM THINK:

What an idiot!

It would all change if Phil's wife would just say, "John, would you come over and show Phil how to run the vacuum cleaner? He's having a terrible time with it, and women are just no good at explaining things."

JOHN:

Oh, okay. Sure.

PHIL THINKS:

Huh? I know how to run a vacuum, for heaven's sake. I don't need John coming over!

THE MEN IN THE ROOM THINK:

Whoa, Phil, you're a loser.

THE WOMEN IN THE ROOM THINK:

Hey, it worked!

After the party, Phil will complain to his wife that she made him feel foolish. It will be tempting to observe that "foolish" might actually be a pretty good word for a person who can't master a sweeper, but if she were to innocently point out that, well, he just seemed to be experiencing such difficulty that he needed John's help, he'll get all huffy and insist that next time he'll prove to her he darn well can use a vacuum cleaner!

In the world of con men, this is known as a "reverse."

EVEN WHEN THEY HELP, THEY'RE NOT MUCH HELP

Even if Dr. Richards were to risk his connective tissues to prepare dinner, he wouldn't actually prepare dinner. Men have a certain perspective on the issue of what work goes into the making of a meal, illustrated here by a list of tasks associated with the preparation of a simple meal of steak, salad, and scalloped potatoes.

PREPARING A MEAL WITH A MAN'S "HELP"

WOMAN TASKS	MAN TASKS
Plan the meal.	
Purchase the food.	
Set the table.	
Wash the vegetables.	
Slice and chop the vegetables and put in a salad bowl.	
Peel the potatoes.	
Boil the potatoes.	
	(continued)

PREPARING A MEAL WITH A MAN'S "HELP" (continued)

WOMAN TASKS	MAN TASKS
Slice the potatoes and sauté them in butter. Whip butter, milk, and flour into a white sauce. Place potatoes in pan, layered with white sauce and cheese. Sprinkle breadcrumbs and garlic powder on top of the potatoes. Bake the scalloped potatoes. Time the potatoes so as to be ready when the steaks are.	Grill the steaks.

After the meal, ask the man to help with the dishes, and he'll be indignant. "What?" he'll demand. "But I cooked dinner!"

Notice how I said "help" with the dishes. To a man, housework is something he helps with, not something he actually does. Furthermore, he usually feels that the most assistance he can provide is in the area of supervision, rather than in an area a woman might find actually helpful, like work.

Men see a household as a corporation—they are the CEOs with command authority and executive perks, and the women are the executive perks. Men feel most productive when they are standing around watching a woman work and are providing observations that begin with the delightful statement, "You know what you should do . . ."

TIP Here's how to handle this situation.

WOMAN:

(trying to arrange the refrigerator so that the leftovers will be good for something besides compost) This doesn't fit.

MAN:

You know what you should do . . .

WOMAN:

(interrupting) No, why don't you show me?

MAN:

Well, um . . .

Try this a few times and the man will learn to keep his mouth shut.

Also keep in mind that housework doesn't sound very masculine to him. Subtly change your vocabulary, identifying the tasks you want him to undertake as trash disposal engineering or managing his spouse. Also play to his masculine nature with statements like this:

"Would you mind vacuuming the house? I think the sweeper is about to explode!"

"I'm terrified of the laundry, would you fold it?"

"Could you do the dishes? I think the garbage disposal is really a ravenous creature named Glork from the planet Quork!" (If you use this one, make sure the silverware is put away first.)

Don't worry if these statements make you sound, well, completely deranged. Most men will fall for them anyway. Helping women in distress is what men do; it makes us hold in our stomachs and stand with our capes flapping in the breeze.

HOW MEN ORGANIZE HOUSEWORK SO THAT THEY CAN IGNORE IT MORE EASILY

Men believe that laundry, mail, tools, and other common household items are best organized in shapeless, shifting stacks called "piles." Everything is there when you need it, and piles can serve dual purposes: for example, a stack of clean towels makes for a handy footstool.

Piles also possess an almost magical quality: They are invisible to the male eye.

Here's a scientific experiment that will prove this theory.

A Scientific Experiment

Materials needed: A man, a staircase, a stack of his freshly cleaned laundry that includes several "favorite" T-shirts.

Experiment: Set the pile of clean male laundry on the stairs.

Observations: Make note of the number of times the man climbs past the clean clothes without picking them up. Don't point out to him that as long as he is walking right past the laundry it wouldn't kill him to carry something up the stairs though if you do it really won't make any difference. Also record the frequency with which the man asks you where he might find his favorite T-shirt, which is in plain view in the pile.*

Conclusion: Piles are invisible.

---

*Do not tell the man where he can actually find the T-shirt. Tell him it must be in the laundry, and invite him to go in and run a load himself. He'll quickly lose interest in the subject.

Men also believe that utilizing piles can free human beings from the trammels of conventional decorating. A dining room is thus a perfect place for piles of fishing equipment, particularly if the look is balanced by the artful placement of a bag of golf clubs in the corner.

Training a man to acknowledge the existence of piles is rather simple: Take something he needs and bury it inside the pile, so he's forced to plunge his hands in there to find it. Be sure to pick something vital to his very existence, like the TV remote, and not something he can live without, like his toothbrush. Pretty soon, you'll start having conversations like this:

HIM:

(standing in the family room) Honey, I can't find the TV remote. I feel like I've lost my purpose in life. (This may not be what he says, but it's how he feels.)

YOU:

(from the kitchen) Did you check the couch?

HIM:

(stares at couch) I can't find it!

YOU:

Look in the pile of stuff on the couch!

HIM:

You had it last!

YOU:

Did you look in the pile of stuff on the couch?

HIM:

I can't find it!

YOU:

It's in the pile of stuff on the couch.

HIM:

I can't find it!

YOU:

Check the pile of stuff on the couch!

HIM:

(a little ticked off, since it would be so much easier if you would just come in and find it for him) All right.

YOU:

Did you find it?

HIM:

(a bit amazed—where before there was nothing, suddenly he sees a pile of stuff on the couch) Hey!

YOU:

Did you find it?

HIM:

I found the remote! It was in this pile of stuff on the couch!

Of course, once you've trained him to spot piles, you've accomplished the same thing all women accomplish when they set out to remodel a man: nothing.

A PRACTICAL EXERCISE IN REMODELING A MAN: SOCKS IN FRONT OF THE HAMPER

When a man becomes aware of the piles around the house, he generally goes into detective mode, believing it will be most helpful if he can determine who is guilty of creating the problem. His investigation will be driven by a certain amount of self-righteousness, a moral crusade to indict someone beside himself.

Sometimes his sleuthing will turn up nothing, because there are some piles that seem to form of their own volition—meaning, the man made them. A good example of this are the balls of socks lying in front of the open hamper, as if they had been washed up by the tide.

A woman might observe that it would take no more effort to place these socks inside the hamper than to put them on top of or in front of the hamper, but that is missing the point entirely. For a man, the inside of a hamper is symbolic of commitment. Once banished to the hamper's dark interior, socks and T-shirts and other items are irretrievably in the laundry. However, as long as the socks haven't yet been tossed in to mingle with other people's stuff, they have the potential of being recalled for active duty. A quick sniff to determine if they are still fresh enough to use and a man can don them for another day.

TIP If you are vexed by small piles of socks, here's a solution for you: Above the open hamper, hang a small white board and write your man's name on it. Each time you notice that he has managed to achieve hamper insertion with some article of clothing, write down the item, plus two points, and total the result like this:

T-Shirt	2
Jeans	2
Total Score	4

When he's created a reserve pile of socks in front of the hamper, deduct points from his score, like this:

Socks	−2
Total Score	2

Don't talk to him about what you are doing, because then he'll want to argue about the rules. Be aware that you need to ignore when he starts tossing certain other items into the hamper, like empty beer cans or the dog bowl. No points for those: This is strictly about the laundry.

If his interest starts to flag, motivate him by saying things like this: "I just talked to Lydia, and her husband's score is up to a hundred and forty-six. I told her I thought you'd do a lot better than that, even if you are only at nine." Pause for a moment to let your comment sink in, then remark, "Wow, a hundred and forty-six points . . . imagine what he'll get for that!"

Sometimes this point system will fail you, particularly if the man in question has a habit of disrobing whenever and wherever he happens to be when he thinks it is time to change clothes. Many women feel there are appropriate places to take off clothing, for instance, the bedroom, and inappropriate places, like the garage. Men, however, don't always recognize these designations, so piles of dirty clothes will start to build up whenever they are in the kitchen and conclude it's too hot to be wearing a shirt, or are in the living room and decide their underpants are "itchy."

The solution to this problem is obvious: simply place a clothes hamper in every room. They are inexpensive and are marvelously handy for hiding stuff when you're trying to pick up the house in a hurry.

TIP ⟩ If your taste in home decorating is less hamper-centric and more, well, good, try this every time you spot an article of clothing lying where your man dropped it: spray it liberally with furniture polish and use it to wipe down some shelves. When you're finished, be sure to put the thing right back where you found it. Pretty soon, when he starts hunting around for some cast-off sweatshirt to put back on, he'll notice that everything he owns smells like Lemon Pledge.

"Hey," he'll complain, "did you do something to my sweatshirt? It's got lemon dust all over it."

"What?" you should respond. "I'm sorry, it was just lying on the floor. I thought it was a rag."

Repeat this process until he either figures out that to prevent you from using his clothing to polish furniture, he needs to hide it from you in the hamper, or you've ruined everything he owns, and he walks around all day with a towel wrapped around his waist. Either way, you've eliminated piles!

THIS IS GOING TO WORK!

Right off the bat you can see how valuable this book is going to be, and why I'm probably going to be voted out of my gender for having written it. First, as you suspected all along, I revealed to you that men are deliberately bad at housework. We pretend to be unable to muster the intelligence required to iron a shirt, though we still think only men should be president.

Then I demonstrated a way to turn a man's very nature against himself, getting him so involved in racking up sock points that he forgets the most important thing is to pretend he can't figure out how to use a laundry hamper.

Of course, some men don't need this type of training. They don't need to be remodeled, because they already do their fair share of the housework, and if they see a sock in front of the hamper, why, they pick it up and put it inside, and sometimes they even take the hamper to the laundry room and do a load of whites. These males are known as Men Who Are with Other Women. Since you don't have one of these yourself, you're going to need all of my tips and techniques to remodel your man.

Read on.

3.

- - -

SPORTS

Both a Metaphor and a Substitute
for Real Life

Lots of women enjoy athletic competition, though they seem to believe that when you get right down to it, sports are nothing more than just a bunch of games. For men, sporting events are the equivalent of real history, having the same world significance as when Columbus explained to the people living in America that he had discovered them. This is patently ridiculous: As a Changed Man, I realize that sports can hardly be considered to have earth-shaking impact, unless we're talking about the Superbowl or maybe Wimbledon.

Yet some women seem to believe that all they have to do to re-model a man's obsession with sports is point out that there is something irrational about standing shirtless in a snowstorm with "Go Packers!" written in green and gold greasepaint across one's stomach, and the man will say, "Whoa! You're right! This is stupid! Let's talk about our feelings!"

Oh sure, there are women in the stadium, standing in the freezing rain in Eastern Wisconsin, screaming and waving and appearing less than rational themselves, but are they shirtless? Of course not. A man can always act more stupid than a woman. It's one of his principal skills.

Men believe that sports stars are like superheroes. They have amazing powers and wear cool outfits. If a man is obsessed with sports, he feels he is actually involved with the team—it's like being an honorary member of the Justice League of America.* This makes him a hero, too! So the problem is, when you ask a man to stop pretending he has an active role on his favorite sports team, it's a little like telling him he needs to quit fighting crime with Batman.

In order to remodel a man, you must break down the barrier between the sexes and see sports the way he does. Think not like a man: just think not.

SPORTS TALK: A LANGUAGE ALL ITS OWN

The best way to beat the Dolphins is to outscore them.

—JOHN MADDEN, football commentator
and former NFL coach

Men see themselves as active creatures, full of ambition and energy that need to be channeled into physically competitive outlets,

---

*The Justice League of America is made up of Superman, Batman, the Flash—people like that. So you can see why it would be so cool to be invited to join them.

like sitting in a recliner all weekend watching other people exercise. Observe a man shouting at the television on any given game day and you realize that it is through sports that restless, unhealthy feelings of frustration and anger are directed safely into less harmful emotions, like annoyance and fury.

This effect is enhanced when men gather in tribal groups to watch the games together. They express enjoyment in the form of loud swearing and eat salt in the form of potato chips. It's obnoxious and uncivilized, but that's pretty much the point; if we were dainty and punctilious, we wouldn't be heroic men.

Imagine me sitting with my friends, watching a game on television and acting civilized, and you'll see how quickly the fun goes out of it.

ME:

I say, didn't the gentleman in pursuit of the receiver commit a most grievous foul by enfolding a handful of jersey in his closed fist at precisely the moment the football was airborne?

FRIEND #1:

By Jove, Bruce, I do believe that a review of the television transmission, with the motion slowed to provide extended opportunity to examine the event, lends unimpeachable support to your observation.

FRIEND #2:

Do allow me to differ, my good man. Clearly, your vision is muddled from having your head in your alimentary canal.

ME:

Forsooth!

FRIEND #1:

Nay, honorable sir, I submit to you that if you cannot see that which is so plain on the screen, you are most likely suffering from an intestinal backup, which has rendered your eye color brown.

> ME:

Gentlemen, may I ask that you clear the viewing area, so that I may recommence my enjoyment of the contest of football before me?

Okay, even as a Changed Man, I can assure you men just aren't going to talk like this. Here's a much more likely conversation.

> ME:

Whoa!

> FRIEND #1:

That's in there.

> FRIEND #2:

Yeah!

> ME:

Did you . . . Did you see that? Did you *see* that?

> FRIEND #1:

That was *in* there!

> FRIEND #2:

Yeah!

> ME:

Oh man! Oh man oh man! Did you see that?

> FRIEND #1:

Baby!

> FRIEND #2:

Yeah!

ME:

I mean . . .

FRIEND #2:

Yeah!

FRIEND #1:

In there, baby. Yes!

FRIEND #2:

Yeah!

ME:

I mean . . .

FRIEND #2:

Yeah!

ME:

I mean . . . Did you, oh man, did you see that?

FRIEND #1:

That was *in* there, baby.

FRIEND #2:

Yeah!

In this instance we sound as if we are speaking a language that has evolved for the express purpose of preventing communication. In reality we are saying something very profound to each other: *Hey, we're on the team!*

SPORTS TALK IN THE WORKPLACE: AN IMPORTANT ELEMENT IN THE ONGOING EFFORT TO WASTE TIME

Men used to be in charge of just about all businesses, but that changed when women showed up and started displaying the one feminine characteristic that males find so irritating in women: competency. Companies responded to the influx of female workers by changing their structures to be based more on merit and less on ego. This was threatening to men, who felt like this new system was far more cumbersome and difficult to manage, what with all the increased profits and everything. So they reacted defensively, bringing the language of sports talk into the workplace.

Whenever men have a meeting at work, they start off with a discussion of some current sporting event. This is how men (a) break the ice, and (b) show off for the women in the room.

Sometimes the meeting opener extends itself into stories of personal triumph on the sports field. Men always listen very respectfully when other males are bragging about some accomplishment in high school or even grade school. The rule is, if you listen without interruption you'll get a turn to tell your own story. Women often convey with their expressions the impression that they would much rather talk about which article should run on page one than sit through a second retelling of a water polo match from the ninth grade, so it should come as no surprise that women are rarely invited to share their stories.

They pretend that this doesn't bother them, but it *must*.

I am a Changed Man on this issue, due to an unfortunate incident that occurred during an editorial meeting at my newspaper. It was my turn to present a personal sports story, and I was enthralling the attendees with a recounting of my heroic role in a key play in a high school football game, when I was rudely interrupted by an editor whose identity I'll protect by calling her Big Mean Gloria.

"This was your sophomore year of high school, you say?" Big Mean Gloria blurted obnoxiously, just as everyone was leaning forward in rapt attention to hear how I deftly slipped past two offensive linemen who were unable to face down my gritty determination. (This is exactly how I put it, "gritty determination," which gives you a pretty good idea of what an exciting story it was.)

I carefully did not allow my annoyance to show. "Hey, shut up, I'm telling a spellbinding story here," I said kindly.

But she persisted, as if perversely determined to ruin everyone's morning. "And you went to Shawnee Mission East High School."

"Yes, that's right, Gloria," I responded in clipped tones.

Big Mean Gloria shoved the speakerphone into the center of the table. "Good. Coach?"

"I'm here," came a distinctly gruff voice. I began to get a very bad feeling from all of this.

"Gloria, I'm not sure this is the best time . . ." I started to say.

"That you, Cameron?" queried the gruff voice.

"Coach Thurgood?" I replied in disbelief.

"Your friend has been filling me in on some of the horse manure you've been dishing out. I've never heard such nonsense in my life."

"She's . . . she's not my friend," I rebutted cleverly.

"What's this about you sacking the quarterback, picking up the fumble, and running it in for the winning touchdown in the final seconds of the district championship game? Don't you think I'd remember something like that?"

I glanced at my friend Sarah. Her face revealed the same horror I felt: The man had clearly lost his mind.

"Coach, I realize it has been a long time . . ."

"The year you played was the worst season I had. I still have the team picture," he stormed. "We're all looking upset with our last-place standing, and then there's you in the middle of the photograph with your spotless uniform, grinning like an idiot."

I could think of nothing to say.

"Coach, thanks so much for taking the time with us this morning," Big Mean Gloria simpered. She reached out a talon and clicked off the telephone.

I slapped my forehead. "Wait, there was this other guy on the team, also named Cameron . . ."

"Gentlemen," Gloria interrupted, "does anyone else have any stories to tell, or can we get to work?"

There was a long silence. I looked over at Sarah, but she was as shocked by Big Mean Gloria's behavior as anyone else. She appeared so tense she seemed ready to burst into an anxious giggle.

"Rodney?" Big Mean Gloria suggested, turning her evil glare on a coworker who often told of a stellar career as a high school soccer player. "You went to Central High, right? Class of 'eighty-five?"

Rodney turned pale, mutely nodding.

"Do you have a story for us, Rodney?" Big Mean Gloria hissed softly, ignoring what I am sure was the unified hatred of everyone else in attendance.

Rodney shook his head.

"Okay, then," Big Mean Gloria concluded smoothly, "let's quit wasting time."

We went on with the meeting at that point, the women all chattering about some inconsequential stuff like upcoming features assignments while the men sat in deathly silence. When our dazed eyes met, we exchanged a clear message: We'd learned an important lesson and would never again make the mistake of opening a business meeting with sports stories when there was a speakerphone in the room.

WHEN MEN SHOUT
AT THE TELEVISION

My older daughter is very proud of the fact that she is out of school, working downtown, and living in her own apartment, which she shares with several other girls who are aspiring models. Though beautiful, they are all so thin I'm afraid if I bump into one of them her hips will give me a puncture wound. I call them the young and the breastless.

Since her roommates are attempting to live a life free of food, my daughter will often drop by my place for a meal. These are usually unplanned visits and are actually a real treat for me: She'll come over to my place, put her clothes in my washing machine, fix herself a sandwich, pour herself a soft drink, and sit with me to reflect on how different her life is now that she is an independent adult. Oh, and would it be okay for her to have some friends come over and watch my TV, she wants to know.

"Sure," I tell her.

"Great! Well, I have to go, when my clothes are done would you mind folding them, and I'll swing by to pick them up later? Oh, and I need to remember to bring your vacuum cleaner back!"

My vacuum cleaner has been out on loan for so long I bought another one.

I rarely am invited to her place, probably because she doesn't want me to notice that she still has possession of my blender. So it came as a bit of a surprise when she accused me one day of "never coming over."

Apparently, this is how she had decided to phrase her invitation to dinner.

"It will be just you, me, and my sister," she told me.

We set the date for Monday night, which didn't cause me any

concern because though her television was small, she had cable. I arrived at her apartment just before kickoff.

"Did you bring the salad?" my older daughter greeted me. She is tall for a woman and has my athletic ability, which is why she was an all-state volleyball player. She's beautiful and fun and witty: I'm proud of her and feel that she is living proof of the old expression that "People turn out well when they have amazing fathers."

"Here," I said, handing her the package. "Also the other items you asked me to pick up."

It took several trips to haul in the "few things" she requested I bring over.

My younger daughter was on the telephone talking to her friends, managing what they term in the telecom business "unusually high call volume." She waved at me. She's extremely popular and outgoing—I did a good job raising her, too.

I turned on the game.

"Hey," my older daughter objected. "What are you doing?"

"What do you mean?"

"I thought we could have a quiet dinner, just the three of us," she explained.

"It is quiet, honey," I explained. "I've got the sound off. Oh . . . THAT'S PASSING INTERFERENCE!"

"Dad," my younger daughter hissed, her hand over the receiver. "Do you mind?"

"Sorry, but I have to throw a flag on this one," I fumed, grabbing a tissue from the box and tossing it to the floor.

My older daughter stared at me as if I had just done something crazy.

My younger daughter hung up. "Dad, we wanted to spend time with you, we never talk. Oh, just a minute—" she interrupted herself as her cell phone rang again.

"We want to get to know you better," my older daughter affirmed.

"I thought you just invited me over so I could visit my blender."

"Please," she said in deadly patient tones.

"Well okay, then—OH HE WAS OFFSIDES—let's talk—OH COME ON! OFFSIDES!"

"With the TV on?" she pressed.

"You want to get to know me better, don't you?" I challenged.

"Well yeah, but . . ."

"Well it's *Monday Night Football.* LOOK AT THAT PASS HE'S GOING . . . HE'S GOING . . . OH WHAT DO YOU MEAN, 'HOLDING'? THERE WAS NO HOLDING!" I protested.

My younger daughter was off the telephone. "What's all the yelling?" she asked, but when I explained that you're allowed to block with your arms as long as you don't actually grab the defensive lineman, her eyes glazed over.

"So did your date for Saturday cancel?" my older daughter asked.

"No. I'm going to the party with Barry, but then John is taking me out for breakfast," my younger daughter replied.

"Would you two hush?" I interjected lovingly.

They turned on me. "You've got the sound off," my older daughter objected.

"Yes, but your talking is distracting me."

They looked at the screen. "Dad, it's a beer commercial."

"It's my favorite beer commercial!" I countered.

They rolled their eyes. "How come you're allowed to shout, but we can't even carry on a normal conversation?"

"What do you mean? I'm watching the game."

They left the room, and I turned up the volume.

A few minutes later they were back, sitting down and looking oddly tense. I glanced at them, but felt that my team needed my help concentrating on a critical third and four situation. The ball was snapped.

"HE'S RUNNING WITH THE BALL!" my older daughter shouted.

"NOW HE'S THROWING IT TO THE OTHER GUY!" my younger daughter yelled back.

"OH NOOOOOOO!" they screamed in unison when the pass was bobbled. My younger daughter threw the box of Kleenex to the floor. "I'm declaring a foul ball," she stated emphatically.

"Is there some kind of point you're making here?" I asked testily.

"QUIET, IT'S MY FAVORITE CAR COMMERCIAL," my older daughter boomed.

"HE'S DRIVING THE CAR ON A MOUNTAIN ROAD!" my younger daughter screeched.

"IT'S GETTING MUDDY IN THE RIVER!" my older daughter rejoined.

"OH NOOOOOOO!"

After about five minutes of this, I moodily turned off the television, a Changed Man on the subject. From then on, when my daughter invited me over for dinner, I would first make sure there were no games on.

"Should I tell him now?" my older daughter asked her sister.

My younger daughter bit her lip.

As the father of two girls, I naturally assumed that whatever they were about to say was going to be so awful it would kill me. My mind flashed to several scenarios, many of which involved me suffering an attack of premature grandfather syndrome. "Tell me what?" I gasped weakly.

My older daughter leapt up and left the room, returning a minute later holding a small bundle of black fur. "I need you to take care of Mittens for me," she said, holding out a kitten for my inspection. The cat, who was jet black save four little white paws, scowled at me.

"What are you talking about? Mittens?" I replied, dumbfounded. "What mittens?"

"It's Mittens the kitten," my younger daughter explained.

"We can't have a cat here in my place, it's against the rules, and we got caught. I need you to watch Mittens for me until I move somewhere else," my older daughter said.

"I thought you have a year lease," I objected.

"Right, just a year. Until I move to a place that takes cats."

Now, I love every kind of animal on the planet, but not cats. It's not my fault; cats don't like me, either. I have always felt that cats prefer the company of women, while canines prefer the company of anyone with a dog treat in their pocket. Yes, I wanted to become a Changed Man, but not at the expense of living with a cat.

My older daughter dropped Mittens, and it scampered off. "Out of the question," I responded firmly. "I'm not having a cat. I don't like cats."

When I took Mittens home that night, I set up the litter box in a spare cupboard and put out an old pillow for it to sleep on. Mittens wandered my apartment, sniffing suspiciously, while I fell asleep wondering who won the game.

YOU, TOO, CAN HAVE SUPER POWERS

Men usually appreciate having women in the room when they are watching sports, and they call these women "waitresses." If they are at home, men generally would like the same level of service to be available to them as in a sports bar, and too often, women find themselves complying with what seems to be a reasonable request for more pretzels or beer without considering the larger implication: There's no tipping!

TIP〉 As an alternative to turning yourself into a waitress, remember that the original Justice League had a female superhero: Wonder

Woman. Now, I'm not suggesting you dress in a Wonder Woman outfit next weekend, though if you do I imagine your man would turn off the television in a hurry. Instead, try this: The next time a game is on, turn to your man and say, "Honey, get me a beer, would ya?"

Chances are, he'll be too flabbergasted to say no. Then hit him with a comment like this: "The way this player swings reminds me a little of Barry Bonds, and his batting average is the same as Bonds's second year, two sixty-one. Though I doubt he'll ever achieve Barry's fifty-nine RBIs."

He'll be dumbfounded. By inserting yourself directly into the sport your man is watching, you are exploding the precious myth that his favorite pastime is something that women will just never understand, and that he is protecting some sort of sacred trust when he sits in his chair and gazes rapturously at an advertisement for Chevy trucks.

During the beer commercial, when he seems to be regaining some of his balance, mute the sound and challenge him for his opinion on the effect of the air density at Coors Field in Denver on the incidence of home run hits. Roll out some stuff you've memorized about humidity and the effects of day versus evening temperatures on barometric pressures. Don't let him counter with any opinion that isn't backed up with hard science. Every time there is a commercial, bring up some new subject like this, until somewhere in the fourth inning, his eyes will look like a hunted animal's.

Then give him a way out. "Remember when we went on that hike together? I had so much trouble keeping up with you. How come your legs are so much stronger than mine?" Or, "If you have a minute, I'd really like you to figure out for me what's going on in the garden—there seem to be all these weeds, and you're so good at identifying those." Or even, "I've tried and tried to fix the screen door, but I just don't think I'm strong enough. Should we call the Justice League of America?"

Okay, the last one is a little over the top, but you get the drift, here. Pick something that makes him feel both smart and strong.

If you want to reward him later by putting on your Wonder Woman outfit, that will just reinforce the message.

4.

- - -

GETTING HIM INTO
SOME SHAPE OTHER THAN
THE CURRENT ONE

What Was Once Hunk Is Now Chunk

Once a man is married or otherwise "attached," he usually comes to regard the mirror as the most useless appliance in the house.* A single man will check in with his reflection at least occasionally, understanding that his chances of meeting women are drastically reduced if, for example, he has small bits of food clinging to his face. Sometimes his quick inspection will reveal a kernel of corn or a daub of blueberry pie, allowing him to enjoy that oh so masculine delight: Snack on a face! The attached man doesn't need the mirror for anything. If he is rushing out of the house, late for a meeting, he just assumes his hair is combed and

---

*I am aware that, strictly speaking, the mirror isn't actually an "appliance." An appliance is something that a man will break while attempting to fix. A mirror has no electrical cord, which means men don't (a) try to repair it, or (b) consider it to be a good birthday present.

his tie is knotted correctly. If not, he knows his mate will tell him: Married men check their reflections by looking at their wives.

When she asks him, in turn, how she looks, the man will always advise her reassuringly that she looks "fine." This causes her to sigh and go find a mirror, as if he has let her down somehow. Frankly, I think it is rather adorable of men that they can assess a woman's appearance without even glancing in her direction.

Here's what happens in a typical household, revealing the different relationship men and women have with their own reflections.

After scowling at the mirror for several minutes, turning from side to side, (What's the problem, isn't she listening? She looks fine!) a woman will decide she needs more precise feedback.

"Honey," she'll say, stepping into the family room, "do I look fat to you?"

The man, looking up from the television, will gape in horror. Even the most obtuse male knows this is the sort of question he should never answer.

"The Jets just punted," he'll mumble, which is why so many women think men are incapable of spontaneous conversation. It's not that we can't be spontaneous, we just don't know what you want us to say!

Now, just watch a man taking stock of his own reflection—he does enjoy it. He already knows he looks fine. He sucks in his stomach, flexes his muscles, and admires how good he still looks. He doesn't see that his gut is spreading like a glacier carving out a new continent. If all you're going to do is focus on the negative, why even bother looking in the mirror?

The woman, underestimating the deluding effect of all this gut-sucking, honestly believes her man will realistically assess his own body and change his behavior—eat better, maybe do some sit-ups, cut back on beer. She may therefore be surprised when he concludes, after a lengthy interaction with his mirror, that what he really needs is a sandwich.

Distressed, she'll phone her friends and use the "F" word. "He's getting so fat," she'll lament.

"Hey, are we out of peanuts?" he'll call from the other room. Meaning, *Hey, can you bring me some peanuts?*

Eventually it gets so bad, the woman will decide to take action. "I bought you these khakis," she'll say. "I got them in a larger size so they'll fit better."

Well, that's it. Now he'll do something, the woman thinks. *He'll start running or working out at the gym. I just hate that I had to be so obvious about the whole thing.*

The man thinks: *Huh. New pants.*

Okay, perhaps even more direct action is needed. "I see you're getting some love handles," the woman finally observes, putting a playful tone into her voice to take the sting out of what she is saying.

The man processes this statement by picturing the uses to which one might put these "love handles." Sounds pretty good!

The woman, watching his face take on a sly expression she knows all too well, wonders how on earth he could be responding sexually to the news he is getting fat!

Look, if you really want to change a man's physique, you're going to have to fight dirty. Put your moral and ethical qualms aside, and hit him where it counts:

Buy him a toy.

IF I ONLY HAD THE RIGHT EQUIPMENT . . .

It seems to me that when a woman decides to do something, she generally does it. *I need to exercise more,* she'll say to herself, and within five minutes she's on the floor doing leg-lifts. When a man decides to do something, he immediately makes a list of reasons why he can't. Chief among these is the lack of the proper equipment.

I'd work out, he reasons, *but I don't have the right kind of shoes. I'd need a sweatband and a water bottle. I wonder if there is a hockey game on?*

If you want your man to go to war against his own stomach, you need to outfit him for battle. He needs a brand new T-shirt because all the ones in his drawer, even the ones with the holes under the arms, are his "favorite" and he doesn't want to ruin them by sweating in them. New running shoes are a must: Try to find a pair with words like "ultra," "mega," or "nuclear" on the box. Running shorts will complete the outfit, but when you see your man walking around in Lycra, his stomach spilling over the tight waistband and his legs poking out like a stork's, do not laugh; he needs to feel like a warrior.

For most men, owning a lot of new gear is enough of an impetus, but others will simply put "Go running" on their to-do list, which might more accurately be termed the list of things "to don't." I was one of these tough cases myself, so when Sarah, my coworker with the unhealthy fixation on physical fitness, started giving me unsolicited advice on a subject I don't care about, i.e., my longevity, I figured it wouldn't have any impact on me personally. Advice on how to improve yourself is the reason we have the word "ignore." But I underestimated Sarah's resolve—one day, without warning, she showed up at my house with a gadget.

"It's a heart monitor," she advised me as I sat staring blankly at what looked like a large wristwatch. I put it on and, being a man, was immediately gratified when the display lit up. "I got a couple of them for free at a trade show and immediately thought of our 're-modeling a man' project. My theory is that if you saw your heart beating, you might become interested in doing things to make it continue doing so. You'd be remodeled into better shape."

"Heart rate, eighty-seven," I informed her. I stood up. "Eighty-nine," I noted. "That's a two-point difference!"

"You can set it so that when you run, it calculates your average heart rate per mile," she encouraged.

"Great!" I beamed. My brain allowed the phrase "when you run" to slide right past my censors like a couple kilos of narcotics being waved through customs. I should have been incredulous. When I run? When the heck do I run? I don't even walk, but now I have a device that tells me how many beats per mile I am racking up. Per mile? Do you know how far a mile is?*

I didn't register any of this; I was busy pushing the buttons. There was a little light for people whose hearts beat at night, and a way to store the data so that six months from now I could check to see what my pulse rate used to be. Pretty important information!

See how deviously clever this is? "Hey, I'm up to ninety-one!" I shouted with delight from the bathroom. "Eighty-eight," I announced as she left. "Eighty-four," I reported to my younger daughter when she called from college.

"Age or IQ?" she chirped.

A few days later I called Sarah to thank her. "Eighty-seven," I greeted her. "This thing is great!"

"I saw you wearing it at the office," she observed.

"I'm putting on my Total Testosterone running shoes right now!"

"Really? You're going running?" Sarah wanted to know, her voice oh so innocent.

"I can upload data from the monitor to a Web site," I explained. I said good-bye and headed out the door. The heart monitor manual gave step-by-step instructions for stretching and the proper way to begin an exercise program, but I figured that was for people who were out of shape.

I took the dog with me so I'd have someone to listen to my heart rate reports. He strained at the leash like a sled dog, while I huffed behind him. My leg muscles fell into a regular cadence, my breath-

*A mile is so far that in Europe, where countries are smaller, the people have to use kilometers instead, or they'd run completely out of room.

ing came easily. I hadn't really run since John Nunnick threatened to punch me in the nose in sixth grade, but here I was, burning up calories and hitting a very gratifying 119 on my heart monitor. My driveway slants upward and is more than twenty feet long, but I had no problem by the time I reached the end of it. In fact, the only worry I had was that I might "over-train" myself—I've read that this can happen to athletes who aren't careful.

My canine thought the purpose of the whole process was to provide him with an opportunity to chase down squirrels, and immediately dove off after one. I stumbled after him like a water-skier behind a speedboat. "Hey!" I gasped, not enjoying the sensation of having my body collide with tree trunks. The squirrels darted up into the branches and chattered down at us, upset that I had disturbed their forest with my skin abrasions.

Having rid the area of rodents, my dog allowed me to drag him out on the road. Grimly, I headed down the hill, my knees quaking. "One-forty," I gasped at my pet, who glanced back at me, startled at this piece of information. The air sawed in and out of my lungs, every molecule stinging like a paper cut. My vision grew dark. 144. I didn't know how much longer we could keep this up—even my dog was panting now. My muscles were spasming into walnut-sized knots. We were passed by a boy pulling a small red wagon.

Time to quit before I overloaded the heart monitor and broke it. I swung into a friend's driveway and fell against the doorbell. Tom came to the door, an alarmed look on his face. "I need to upload some data," I wheezed at him. "I just ran all the way here."

Tom leaned out and looked at my house. "Why?" he wanted to know.

I mutely showed him my heart monitor, concentrating on extracting oxygen from the air.

Once I'd recovered I demonstrated to Tom how I could calculate my heartbeats per mile, if I had run a mile. We uploaded the data to the special Web site, but were disappointed to see that I would need to provide more inputs before any graphs would appear. "Why don't you just make up some numbers?" Tom wanted to know. (He's not very athletic.)

After he drove me home, I phoned Sarah to let her know what good shape I'd gotten in. "Ninety," I greeted her.

"You've been running all this time? You shouldn't have done so much your first day," she exclaimed.

"Well, it's hardly my first day," I replied. "I used to run all the time before I got my driver's license."

"Still . . . how far did you go?"

"I wasn't exactly running the whole time," I admitted. "Tom and I were watching beach volleyball finals at his house."

"What? I thought you went running! You were watching volleyball?"

"Volleyball *finals*," I corrected. My heart monitor reflected a slight surge in response to her inaccuracy.

"So all you did was go down the street and watch TV."

"The dog was having heat stroke!" I responded defensively. My pet snapped his head around, staring at me in disbelief. "We had to quit."

She said something about doing better "next time," which left me a little puzzled. Hadn't I used the word "quit"? I thanked her again for the toy and went to the hammock. It was time for the "cool down," as described in the manual. "Eighty-six," I informed my dog, who yawned drowsily.

A WHOLE BUILDING OF
THE RIGHT EQUIPMENT

Though I've started wearing my heart monitor whenever I remember—usually I put it on right before going to bed—this is apparently not enough remodeling for my older daughter. She's an athlete, always inviting me to go to the gym with her.

"They have a steam room," she beckons, as if there is something attractive about a small closet full of poached naked men.

"I just don't feel like going today or this year," I tell her.

"But Dad, I'm worried about you. I want to see you live longer."

"I am living longer," I inform her. She sighs in a way that I have come to realize means I am so totally right there is no point in arguing.

Having settled this issue, I am somewhat surprised when she phones me from work one morning to tell me her health club is having a special.

"What would make it the most special is if you would leave me alone on the topic," I tell her.

"Where are you going to be tonight, around seven o'clock?"

"Not at the health club," I answer quickly, seeing where this is going.

She decides to give up and asks about my mittens.

"What?" I demand.

"The kitty. Mittens the kitten. She's so cute," my daughter gushes.

"I don't know. Haven't seen the cat in days," I say gruffly. I push Mittens off my lap so she won't blow my cover.

"What? You mean she ran away? What did you do to her?"

"I didn't do anything to her! No, she didn't run away, she's fine. I just wish that she'd sleep in her own bed."

"Where does she sleep?"

"Practically on my face. If you really want me to live longer, you'd take the cat back so I don't die of feline inhalation."

"That's so *cute*," she says again.

"I have to go, too much cooing," I tell her. We hang up and I regard the cat, who is waiting to be invited to jump back up into my lap. "That was your *real* mom," I tell her.

At 7:00 that evening my doorbell rings. Standing on the stoop is a very pretty woman, wearing small shorts and a tank top. "Mr. Cameron?" she asks, giving me a bright smile.

For a minute I founder, then come up with the correct answer. "Yes," I say hesitantly.

She holds out a hand. "I'm Tanya, from the health club? Your daughter said you wanted to join up during our special promotion."

The last thing I want to do is give my time to a salesperson so she can try to sell me something I've never wanted. "Please come in," I tell her. I invite her to sit down, though I'm careful not to be too friendly or to imply she's going to be allowed to stay very long. She declines my offer of a soft drink, iced tea, or to cook her a roasted chicken. Then I break it to her: "Sorry, but I think you wasted your time coming out here. I've told my daughter this before. I would never go, I just don't have time in my schedule."

Tanya glances at my television, where I have muted the show *America's Wackiest Violent Criminals.*

"I know she means well, but I'm just not interested," I continue. "Sorry, but I don't want to join."

"Oh, but you really should," Tanya pouts. "Please?"

I sign up for a three-month trial membership, which includes personal training. Since Tanya is a personal trainer, I'm anticipating that we'll be working together—she certainly implies this will be the case. (She obviously finds me very attractive.)

However, when I arrive at the health club the next day, Tanya is working with some other man, and I am introduced to Fred. Fred's a twenty-ish fellow, taller than I am, with an unhealthy leanness to him. His muscles are bunched in cramped clots as he moves, and I can see the veins sticking out on his arms in what is surely a sign of some horrible debilitation. He also smiles too much, perhaps in a pitiful social response to what is mostly likely universal revulsion to his bumpy physique.

"Bruce, how about we run through a circuit of the weight machines, do a little cardio, and then see how you feel?" Fred enthuses, picking up a clipboard.

I clear my throat. "I understand you have a steam room?"

"Hey, Dad!" my older daughter calls. She leaves a group of people who are jumping up and down in synchronized spasms and comes over to grin at me. She is wearing an outfit that any father would disapprove of, a sports bra much too revealing for a coed environment.

"You're sweating," I advise her severely. "You should put on some bulky sweat clothes."

"Fred, take good care of my dad," she says, giving my arm a friendly squeeze.

"Oh, we will," Fred promises.

I hate it when people with clipboards think of themselves as more than one person.

Fred leads me over to a device designed to yank people's arms out of their shoulder sockets. "This is a pull-down," he explains, sitting on a narrow seat and, well, pulling down. "Okay, now you try it."

"But you're doing so well," I say.

I sit down and reach up for the handles. Biting my lip, I yank downward. There is a popping sound as my spine shatters.

"Okay, wait. Wait," I say. "That hurt."

"What hurt?"

"When I did that, it hurt."

"But where did it hurt?"

"What do you mean, where? My body, Fred, you're hurting my body."

"Did it hurt when you reached up . . ."

"Yes."

"Or when you pulled down . . ."

"Yes."

"Or when you let the bar return to its original position?"

"Yes, thank you. Probably not a good idea for me to start on this particular machine. Where did you say the steam room was?"

"Well let's . . . Okay, let's move to the bench," he suggests.

I'm barely able to get comfortable in this next position before Fred urges me to push on the metal bar over my head. "I thought you were big on pulling, now you want me to push," I snap irritably.

"Just go ahead and lift slowly. Go ahead, Bruce. A little faster. Push. Bruce, are you even pushing? Try to lift the bar."

I throw everything I have into raising the bar from my chest and am awarded with the sensation of my muscles shredding. "Keep going, Bruce! Do as many as you can," Fred urges.

Up and down the bar goes. My blood pounding in my head, I do rep after rep after rep, each one more difficult than the one before. "That's three!" Fred shouts from somewhere in the red haze that has filled my vision.

I catch sight of Tanya, walking up to see how I am doing. I give a last heave, raising the bar one last time. "Twenty-four!" I call out, letting the mechanical arm drop back into place with a crash.

"You should really lower the bar slowly," Fred chides.

Since I am not personally responsible for gravity, I choose to ignore this complaint. "Hi Tanya," I say. I sit up, proud that I can do so without wincing. She's rather stunning, in a tight-fitting sports bra.

"Hi Bruce, you're certainly . . . sweaty," Tanya notes.

"Been working pretty hard here. Sort of pushing Fred to push me," I reply modestly.

Tanya tells me she will see me around, and I turn back to Fred. After an hour we've been to nearly every machine in the club. Fred seems frustrated that due to the way my body is constructed, there is a bad match between me and his infernal devices. "I think maybe I just require a club geared to a more rarified clientele," I comfort him as he gazes sadly at his clipboard.

I finish in the steam room, my aching muscles relaxing under the waves of heat. When I leave, my daughter is waiting for me in the lobby.

"Did you have fun?" she asks eagerly.

I cock my head. "Fun? No, that's not the word I would use. I would say I had 'pain.'"

"What part didn't you like?"

"I'd say that it would have to be a toss-up between the joint dislocation and the internal hemorrhaging."

She links an arm through mine. "We could meet here every evening, if you'd like."

"Wouldn't it be more fun to just go somewhere and have oral surgery?"

We stroll some more. It is ridiculous how far away our cars are located—they really should consider valet parking for people who don't like to walk to their workouts. Glancing at my daughter, I ponder how I'm going to tell her I've decided to quit the club. I know this means a lot to her and I don't want to hurt her feelings. "Well, listen. I have to tell you, I've decided I don't want to be a member of your stupid club," I finally say gently.

"Really?" She stops and turns to look at me, her eyebrows raised in surprise. "Tanya will be sorry to hear that."

Now it is my turn to stop. "Really?"

My daughter nods. "She thinks you're cute."

"Oh. Well," I grunt. "She's a little too young for me, I'd say. I'd hate to break her heart."

"Oh my God no, she is like so much older than she looks," my daughter corrects me. "Her son is in college, even. I mean, she is plenty old enough for someone like you. Did you think she was like in her twenties or something? That would be gross."

I sort through this statement carefully, wondering why I'm having difficulty feeling better. "I really think her age is irrelevant," I say gruffly. "The important thing is whether she is a good trainer. That's what this is about."

"Oh yes," my daughter agrees solemnly.

"You don't join a health club just because an aerobics instructor allegedly says you're cute."

"I guess not."

"I'm pretty sure you made it all up anyway," I state, hoping she'll repeat the words "Tanya thinks you're cute" a few more times.

At her car, I arrange to meet her back at the health club the next evening. Perhaps Fred will have the night off or will have been picked up on an outstanding warrant or something.

YOU CAN FOOL ALL OF
THE PEOPLE ALL OF THE TIME
IF THE PEOPLE ARE MEN

When I tell people I work out on a regular basis, they nearly always react the same way, looking me up and down and saying, "Really? You work out?" in a tone of disbelief. Apparently everyone sees me as the sort of person who is just born with an excellent physique, and doesn't have to go to the gym on Tuesdays, Thursdays, and Fridays—the nights when Tanya works.

Admittedly, I don't work out on a regular basis because I've been very busy, but I have managed to make it every time the club has had a wine and cheese party. If you want to remodel your man, manipulating him the way my daughter is manipulating me is actually very easy.*

---

*A clear demonstration of this can be had in any restaurant. Watch a man's reaction when a cute waitress comes to the table. It may make you sad to see it, but the man assumes the waitress likes him. Here's a pretty, vivacious, smiling woman who banters in a friendly fashion and brings him food. The fact that there is a tip involved doesn't even register on the male brain, which is busy attempting to come up with witty comments to make about the salad dressing.

As a Changed Man, I can see what my daughter is up to. She thinks she's fooling me, but I know that Tanya doesn't lie awake at night thinking about me. When my daughter says that Tanya asked about me, I don't race up to the health club that afternoon—I wait until the next day. This is the downside to remodeling your man; he won't be as easy to fool. I'm onto my daughter's little game, and wouldn't even bother to go to the health club at all, except that, well, Tanya did say I was cute.

That has to mean something, doesn't it?

5.
- - -

MANNERS AND HABITS
AND HYGIENE

Tips on Remodeling a Man So That
He Goes from Being Offensive
to Being Merely Irritating

I may be a Changed Man, but I am still a man, with male sensibilities around manners and habits. If you want to remodel a man, you must first appreciate the difference between the sexes doesn't necessarily imply, as I once believed, that one side is always right and that her side is always wrong.

An event this past summer reveals the complexity of the situation. My next-door neighbors, Tom and Emily, were cooking in their backyard. They know how much I love Tom's recipe for barbecued ribs, so I headed over there the minute the delicious odor wafted into the air. When I arrived, the two of them began to communicate with me in a highly socialized fashion, which as an astute observer of the differences between the sexes, I was able to interpret expertly.

When Emily said, "Oh, Bruce. We're . . . we're just getting ready for dinner."

She meant: *You made it just in time!*

And when she said, "We're having the Fergusons over. Tom and I have really wanted to get to know them as a couple."

She meant: *The more the merrier!*

So I said, "Great!"

And then she said, "Tom, he's your friend. Talk to him."

Which meant: *Don't be so rude, offer Bruce a drink!*

Then Tom said, "Hi Bruce. This is sort of a couples' thing, tonight. You know?"

Which meant: *How come you never have a date?*

And when he said, "I'm sorry that we don't have enough to invite you."

He meant: *Just kidding!*

So Emily's method of inviting me might have been more "polite" than Tom's, but his was more direct.

When Tom makes his ribs, he and I usually drape ourselves in plastic bags and sit on wooden chairs in his backyard and Emily eats in the kitchen. Emily is a sensitive woman, who loves her husband and her carpet. She knows how much men like to eat meat with their hands, so she politely makes an excuse of some kind so that the two of us can be alone, saying that watching us eat ribs gives her "extreme nausea."

Then the Fergusons showed up. Juliet Ferguson and I have never gotten along. She's the sort of person who acts as if she is always qualified to give her opinion about local politics just because she is the mayor. Her husband, Hurly, works for a chemical company, so you'd think he'd appreciate the plastic trash bags Tom and I had donned, but he just gave us a supercilious look when we offered him one.

"Suit yourself, Hurly," I shrugged, which is another example of male polite speech. What I meant was, *Okay, but when Tom eats ribs he splatters everything in the kill zone.*

We sat down on our wooden chairs, Hurly shooting mournful

looks over his shoulder at the two women in the kitchen, and dug into the pile of food.

"Please pass the potato salad," Hurly enunciated, blinking against the steady spray of barbecue sauce.

"You don't have to ask, Hurly, just lunge," I advised kindly.

Tom and I chuckled at the parody of eating Hurly was putting on, taking tiny little bites with his front teeth. Tom's style is to stick the whole rib in his mouth and sort of vacuum the meat off, which usually results in a huge mess that is very gratifying to see. Hurly laughed along with us, but a bit uneasily—probably he was regretting his decision about the trash bag.

"You have a . . ." Hurly gestured toward Tom's cheeks. "A bit of meat, there."

I snorted. "Wait till you see what happens when he eats corn on the cob. By the end of the meal, his face is going to look like a veggie tray!"

Tom grinned through his mask of barbecue sauce. "Hey," he announced brightly. "Hurly. We could call you 'Hurly Davidson.' Pretty funny, huh?"

Now, this was a very friendly and inclusive gesture by Tom, but Hurly didn't seem to get it. In fact, he sort of looked close to crying. Tom and I exchanged glances: We needed to do something to make Hurly feel more at home.

"Hey Tom, why don't you show Hurly that thing you do with deviled eggs," I suggested. And Tom was willing, but Hurly jumped up and told us he wanted to check on his wife, practically running for the kitchen. Baffled, we watched him flee.

I relate this story to reveal a problem with turning someone into a Changed Man: There is a distinct possibility you might over-remodel him. Hurly is a fastidious person, punctilious in manner and speech—in other words, nearly dysfunctional. Tom, on the other hand, is a real man's man, with the largest television of anyone I know.

Clearly, Emily would like to remodel Tom a little, so as to avoid a repetition of his faux pas over not inviting me for dinner. But to avoid winding up with a Hurly, she needs to understand some basic differences between the sexes.

MEN: RAW MATERIAL

Men believe that the definition of manners is "hiding one's habits." This takes a lot of effort, and, as far as a man is concerned, one shouldn't apply effort unless it earns some sort of reward. That's why most men think that good manners are like name tags, useful when you first meet people, but then unnecessary once you get to know them. Why expend all that effort once you've had a few dates, and she knows you and yet is still, for some reason, willing to go out with you?

For example, my uncle Bob cleans his teeth by inhaling sharply with his tongue pressed against them, using air as dental floss. This is pretty clever and not only saves money but is good oral hygiene, in my opinion. According to Aunt Ginny, his wife, he never did this when they were first dating, and she seems more than a little irritated that her husband ends every meal making noises like an air hose. When she talks about this with her women friends, they sympathize with her because they believe this suggests he cared more about my aunt when he was courting her than he does now. To me, it suggests that when he first started dating her Bob walked around with food stuck in his teeth.

Aunt Ginny is fond of announcing, "To say that men are pigs is unfair. To the *pigs*." When she says this, my uncle Bob testily retorts, "Oh, and I suppose it's better that they should become bacon?"

Interesting debate.

Sometimes she attacks from an unexpected direction, switching barn animals right in the middle of the argument. "I wish I'd married a cow, at least I'd get milk out of it," she'll fume.

"Bull," Uncle Bob replies.

You couldn't make up dialogue like that.

Her indictment of her husband has, over time, come to include all men, though she does give "Regis Philburn" a pass because he is "such a handsome man."

"Just look at that Regis, he is such a handsome man," she'll say, fanning herself. "I'm sorry, but if he wanted me to run away with him, I'd go in an instant."

Uncle Bob doesn't seem too worried that this is ever actually going to happen.

HOW TO INCREASE A MAN'S COUTH

My daughters have long and inappropriately been members of the Committee to Reform Dad's Hygiene, taking me to task for my supposed lack of couth. As I understand it, my insufficient couthness has ruined their lives, a process I started when they were teenagers and apparently will never fully complete. For example, they seem incensed that I will occasionally dig a finger deep into my ear, rooting around, and then look at whatever I've extracted. They take me to task for this all the time, but come on, do you really suppose I would pull something out of my ear and not want to see what it was?

And it doesn't end there. "Dad," my younger daughter scolds. "You have got to do something about your nose!"

I have to admit, this one catches me a little off guard. She makes it sound as if my nose has gotten loose and spent the night tipping over the neighbors' trash cans. "Do something about my nose? Like what, remove it?"

"It's gotten really hairy," my older daughter explains.

Alert readers will instantly see the unfairness of this accusation. It's not as if I am growing more hair from my nose on purpose, any more than I am trying to grow less hair on top of my head. It's just happening, a natural migration, like the way geese fly south for the winter if they can't find a golf course.

"I guess I could grow a mustache, sort of comb it all together," I muse innovatively.

"Oh gross!" they shriek in unison.

This one stops me as well. I've had a mustache before and no one complained it was gross, just ugly.

"You can't hide them, you have to pluck them!" my older daughter lectures.

"Or get a bikini wax," my younger daughter adds. They both giggle.

"Pluck?" I sputter, my eyes watering at the very thought. "Obviously you don't have any nose hair yourself."

"Well, obviously," my older daughter sniffs.

"You can't pluck your nose. If you do, the follicle can get infected, and then it has a straight shot to your brain," I pontificate.

"Wait, wait, oh my God," my older daughter gasps. "You're saying you think pulling a nose hair will give you brain damage?"

"Stop laughing, it's true. It's not funny. Get off the floor."

When they have recovered, my older daughter, wiping her eyes, offers an alternative solution. "Well, can you at least trim them?"

I picture trying to manipulate a pair of scissors into such a small and vulnerable place. "With what?"

"I don't know," my younger daughter speculates. "Hedge clippers?"

More hilarity at my expense. I sit with my arms folded, waiting for the hysteria to subside.

In the end, they try to remodel me by getting me a toy, an electric nasal hair trimmer. This shows what happens when you misjudge a man's appetite for gizmos. The nose trimmer is boring: It just buzzes, and eventually induces sneezes so explosive the cat hides under the bed. Nowhere on the device is there a digital read-out—there's no way to keep score. It is not, therefore, a real toy.

As far as I'm concerned, the mustache is the only way to go.

MALE INDUCED INSOMNIA

I do not snore, despite the claims of others to the contrary, but I know how irritating it can be when a person snores and won't admit it. When I worked for the fire department, the firefighters all slept in a room that resembled a prison ward, with cement walls that amplified every sound. The snoring in that room was so loud it kept setting off the motion detectors on the station spotlight. The spotlight had been set up to prevent people from sneaking in and driving off in one of the fire trucks, which can be very embarrassing when it happens. Between the flashing lights and the deep rumbling, it was like trying to sleep in a thunderstorm.

Yet every other man in the place seemed to be able to slumber through the racket, oblivious to the fact that they were being vibrated like guitar strings all night long. Gazing around in wonder, I realized why this was: They were *all* snoring!

> **TIP** If your man snores so loudly you're having trouble sleeping, the best thing to do is teach yourself to snore back in self-defense.

If this doesn't work, there is another way to remodel your man when it comes to snoring. If you are awakened by your man's stertorous breathing, move to the other side of the bed. Then relax into a sleeping position, your face turned away from him. Breathe deeply, letting the tension go out of your body, and shut your eyes. When you are confident you appear fast asleep, take one more deep breath, and then scream as loudly as you can.

Your man will sit bolt upright, clawing at you in alarm. Pretend

he's waking you up, yawning and blinking your eyes crossly, and
have this conversation.

HIM:

What happened? What's wrong?

YOU:

Huh? What are you doing? Why did you wake me up?

HIM:

You screamed!

YOU:

What?

HIM:

You were screaming! It woke me up!

YOU:

That's ridiculous, I wasn't screaming.

HIM:

Yes you were!

YOU:

I do not scream.

HIM:

Yes you do, it's really loud.

YOU:

Well go back to sleep.

HIM:

I can't sleep if you are going to scream!

YOU:

I have to get up early tomorrow for a meeting. Go back to
sleep!

He may never appreciate the subtle irony—men don't really do "subtle"—but his subconscious will be thinking, *Hey, every time we snore, somebody screams and wakes us up! Maybe we should stop!*

Even if his subconscious isn't learning from the experience, the more you repeat this process, the more agitated he'll become, and the more agitated, the less he'll be able to sleep.

And if he's not sleeping, he's not snoring.

A CURE FOR THE WET SANDWICH

A wonderfully male invention is the wet sandwich. This is a meat sandwich so sloppy with sauce or ketchup that it drips like a broken faucet, and must therefore be eaten where broken faucets are kept: over the kitchen sink.

My father used to make the champion of all wet sandwiches, a stack of meatballs, onions, pickles, tomatoes, and, his brilliant addition, bacon, all slathered in so much barbecue sauce that the bread began to disintegrate after the first bite. For some reason, it irritated my mother to watch my father standing at the sink eating, because as she sat at the table, she was forced to converse with his butt. She felt that the two of them should take advantage of the rare break in his work schedule to have a conversation, though in my father's defense, all she seemed to want to talk about were her objections to the wet sandwich.

One summer I accidentally remodeled my father on the topic of his wet sandwiches. I had received a chemistry set for my birthday, and, being an intelligent boy with a precocious scientific curiosity, immediately set about trying to make a stink bomb. The mixture of chemicals I eventually cocktailed did, indeed, stink, though it was less of a bomb than a spill, a wet stain in the backyard. My friends were pretty disappointed at the lack of explosion, though the dog rolled in it appreciatively. The odor was so bad I poured the rest of the batch down the garbage disposal.

When my father leaned over the sink to take his first bite of the wet sandwich, the smell hit him square in the face. Blinking back tears, he ran the disposal, but the odor clung to the air like germ warfare. It was so awful he eventually abandoned his post.

The stench stayed with us all summer, barely noticeable when the sink was dry but always sickening whenever water was poured down the pipes. For some reason, every time my father made himself a wet sandwich, my mother always found reason to run a little water into the mouth of Glork from Quork.

Soon my father would no longer stand at the sink for his wet sandwich, but would sit at the table with my mother, hunks of meat falling to his plate, splattering her with barbecue sauce.

TIP If you find yourself short on toxic chemicals but still want to make your sink unsafe for the wet sandwich, consider soaking clothes in there. Pick something unappetizing, like some old pantyhose you keep in the kitchen just for this purpose. He's not likely to want to move them, and will wind up eating his sandwich somewhere else, like over the dog.

THE MALE BODY AND WHY IT SMELLS LIKE IT IS DECOMPOSING

As a Changed Man, I understand that igniting farts is no longer a funny thing to do, particularly at weddings. This makes me sad, but I know there comes a time in every man's life when he must put away the simple pleasures of childhood, and that time is whenever there are women around.

"I wish you'd talk to your son about setting his gas on fire," my ex-wife complained to me. So I did. "Son," I told him, "it works a lot better with a lighter than with matches. Also, don't do it on the couch."

She also asked me to advise my son to say, "excuse me," whenever he passes gas but in my mind, that's as good as admitting you're the gasser! Besides, I've taught him his whole life that when people are talking and you want to interrupt them, you should say "excuse me" and they will pause and give you their attention. So wouldn't this be like interrupting people so they will pay attention to your fart?

What women don't seem to understand is that men don't make gas on purpose. It comes from the food we eat, and that food is chili.

A CHILI RECEPTION

One evening my children came over to watch a video and to turn down my offers of chili, which I had been cooking and sampling all afternoon. Though pretty full, I felt I had to make a point, so I served myself a large bowl while my kids ordered a pizza.

"Beans are really good for you," I scolded.

"Not when you eat them," my younger daughter informed me.

We started the movie, and I sat there feeling wonderfully bloated and lethargic. Every single internal organ I owned had thrown itself into the effort of processing the chili. My stomach was hissing and gurgling in a manner reminiscent of a Soviet chemical plant. At one point, I leaned forward to grab the remote control, and there was a sound like a pressure tank exploding.

"Dad! Oh my God!" my older daughter screamed, her eyes watering. My son cocked his head at me, clearly wondering where he might have put his lighter.

"Not these," I told him. "I don't want to blow out my windows."

My daughters fled from the room, sobbing. My gastrointestinal tract rumbled like a large truck driving over a wooden bridge. "Could you turn up the volume, Dad?" my son requested. "I can't hear the television over your stomach."

After another blaster even he abandoned me, gasping for breath as he stumbled away. "Could you please open a window?" my older daughter yelled at me from the other room. It sounded like she was holding a blanket over her face.

"And climb through it?" my younger daughter added.

Their outrage seemed a bit overblown to me. It's not as if only the males of the species produce flatulence.

Is it?

I mean, do women fart? And if they don't, what do they do with their gas? Do they store it up all of their lives? I know it is possible to physically close all the valves, so to speak—I've done it in church, turning my buttocks into rock-hard barriers.* But this just delays, and even exacerbates, the inevitable. Apparently the women in my family would never do anything so crass as to vent even a molecule of gas. They must reabsorb all flatulence into their bloodstreams, releasing it later in the form of criticism of me.

Here's what happens to me when I try to contain a gas buildup.

INTESTINE:

Sir! Permission to speak, sir!

BRAIN:

Go ahead, Intestine.

INTESTINE:

Sir, damage report on the burrito we took at eighteen-hundred hours. We are not contained. Repeat, we are not contained. Request emergency venting.

---

*I am not amused by the fact that every single woman who read this statement in draft form noted that the comments about having a rock-hard butt were "not realistic."

BRAIN:

Negative on the venting, we're in church.

INTESTINE:

Sir, we've gone alimentary. We're stretched to the limit. She's going to blow, Captain.

BRAIN:

Hang on, Intestine! We've only got fifteen minutes to go. Buttocks!

BUTTOCKS:

Buttocks reporting, sir!

BRAIN:

We've got a breach from that burrito last night, and it's heading your way. What's your status?

BUTTOCKS:

Buttocks are magnificently rock hard, sir.

BRAIN:

Attaboy, Buttocks. I hope that holds it.

INTESTINE:

Captain, we now have gas pain in sectors two, three, and five, sir.

CAPTAIN:

I'd like to see a woman try to handle something like this!

BUTTOCKS:

Captain sir! All the upstream valves must have failed because our pressure just went off the scales. We're at tolerance, sir, even our exquisitely muscled equipment can't handle this load. I'm afraid we're going to lose it, sir.

BRAIN:

Drat! Buttocks, vent, but try to do so in a controlled fashion. I don't want any noise, if we can help it. Conscience, I want a Guilt Report on my desk in five minutes. Let's see if we can salvage this situation.

HOW TO REMODEL A DOG

Not content with trying to change my behavior, my older daughter also insisted I do something about my dog. "Well good grief, you can't teach a dog not to fart," I protested when I heard my assignment. "How's it supposed to understand something like that?"

"Well," she informed me, "it's very rude when we have company over and the dog passes gas. It's even worse than your chili."

This was a very interesting way to put it, since "we" didn't actually live at *my* house, even though the "company" was usually "her" friends coming over to watch "my" television.

There is nothing in the dog training manual about animal farts, though to be truthful I've never really bothered to read the thing, believing that it's better that dogs should be self-taught than for me to have to expend any effort beyond talking to it when I first brought it home—the "new dog orientation speech." The technique I decided upon was heavy with negative reinforcement: When my pet audibly passed gas, I effected a stern expression on my face, putting my hands on my hips. "Oh, no," I scolded, pointing my finger. "You should never do that, especially when we have company over." I held up photographs of relatives. "See? Company." I then turned and patted my rump. "No gas, no gas." I pantomimed forming rock-hard buttocks and leaving the room. Once out in the hallway, I put on a beatific smile. "Ahh," I said. "Okay to have gas in the hallway. But not where there is company." I held up the photographs again.

The dog absorbed all this with the alert and intelligent expression of, say, a jar of dirt. Clearly I was getting too complicated. "No bad gas," I explained. "Gas . . . no!"

The word "no" seemed to register, and eventually that became the command I settled upon. Whenever my Labrador had flatulence, I would shout "No!" and the dog would lower his eyes and creep from the room. I'm pretty sure he didn't understand what was going on, but he recognized my mood.

We kept at this for several months, and then one day it dawned on him what he had done to cause my wrath. To my delight, he made such a solid connection between his emissions and my anger that it soon became unnecessary for me to say anything: The dog would fart and then slink away in despondent shame.

I was pretty proud of this trick, especially one evening after I'd had a dinner of polish sausage, cole slaw, and baked beans. The kids and I were gathered in the family room, watching television, when I began to feel the beans working their magic. I tried to do what my son calls "run silent, run deep," but instead "went audible."

Hearing the sound, my dog dropped his ears and guiltily eased out of the room.

"That's a bad one," my younger daughter noted for the record.

"Dog gas is the worst," my older daughter agreed.

Probably the best trick I've ever taught an animal: serving as my alibi!

A MAN IS A MAN, A PIG IS A PIG— SEEMS LIKE A PRETTY GOOD SYSTEM TO ME

Suppose we accept for a moment Aunt Ginny's assertion that all men except Regis Philburn are pigs. I might note that pigs can be taught to do a variety of tricks, if you're willing to put the time into training them. There's a nationally famous pig baton twirler, which is interesting because there are no nationally famous *people* baton twirlers. Pigs can be taught to fetch things, which is more than I can say for my dog, and to do a lot of basic pig tricks like sit, roll over, and program a computer. But let's get some perspective here: They're pigs. Sticking them in a cowboy hat and teaching them to twirl a baton does not mean you have done anything but pervert their porcine nature.

Likewise, men can be taught to behave in a way entirely unlike their essential selves. But come on, would that really make you happy? As the old saying goes, "When you want a pig, you want a pig, and when you want a man, you want a man."* The fact that under some circumstances they are relatively interchangeable doesn't alter the undeniable truth of this statement. Pigs can provide companionship, laughter, an unjudgmental ear, and, ultimately, ham sandwiches. Men can help you move furniture. If, in the end, they're a little stinky and hairy (I'm talking about the men, now, not the pigs) isn't it worth it, sometimes?

---

*Okay, this isn't technically an old saying, because I just made it up. But how do you think we get old sayings in the first place? Someone makes them up, that's how.

6.

--- --- ---

COMPETITION

When Men Cut Themselves
on the Competitive Edge

At nearly sixteen, my son is an amazing man-in-progress. He can outgrow a pair of pants in the time it takes to drive home from the store. He eats vast quantities of food to no visible effect other than financial: He can consume an entire pumpkin pie, wash it down with a milk shake, and stand up weighing less than when he sat down.

I often feel that observing him gives me a lens through which to view my own maleness. For example, one afternoon I went to the school to pick him up and was drawn to a small knot of mothers anxiously watching their sons skateboard down some cement stairs. My own child was among them, applying himself with gritty resolve to a sport that to me has about as much appeal as flinging myself naked onto a large sheet of sandpaper.

Observing the skill levels of the participants, I discerned that one of the boarders—a short boy I'll call Psycho—was more practiced than the others, because he displayed the most scabs. Psycho's leaps off the top step were higher than anyone's, and his landings were executed with graceful full-body scrapes on the cement.

I could tell by the look on my son's face that he was determined to beat Psycho at his own game. Powering himself down the sidewalk with ferocious concentration, he soared into the air, lifting his legs off the skateboard. Most of the other boys held on to the board with a hand while they were in the air so they would at least land near the thing, but not my boy. Apparently, my son felt that any successful remounting of the board back on planet Earth was entirely a matter of chance. When his defiance of gravity ended, he crashed like a man tossed from a speeding train.

"That was so stupid," a mother next to me commented.

"He should have grabbed the board in midair," I agreed.

She gave me an odd look, and I immediately understood that she didn't get it. To her, a sport whose primary purpose seems to be to experience pain was one to be avoided, even if some Psycho was better at it than she was. But I understood perfectly what was going on in my son's mind: He couldn't let himself be bested, and wouldn't give up until his body was one continuous abrasion.

I told my son we needed to leave, and though he voiced heavy disappointment, I could see he was a little relieved that he wouldn't have to abandon any more skin on the school steps.

Clearly, men are competitive animals, unwilling to lose a contest even if it's moronic.

Of course, I am a Changed Man. I don't ever indulge in silly rivalries with other men, unless they start competing with me, and then I'll get involved, but only if I am sure I will win. My experiences are instructive for anyone who wants to remodel a man, so it really bothers me when I am falsely accused of being overly competitive, which happened to me recently at the airport, of all places.

I was standing in line at the check-in, hoping I would be lucky enough to upgrade to the "cramp plus" section of the airplane, when I noticed something so odious I felt immediately and completely emasculated: Every other man in my line was talking on his cell phone. Worse, they were all having what sounded like really important business conversations, with references to stuff like "European steel cable shipments" and the "occidental petroleum merger," while my most critical phone call of the past week had been "Who is going to take care of my pets while I am gone?" (My daughters say cats can take care of themselves, but Mittens needs someone to fluff her pillow for her every night.)

My visual survey took me in a complete circle, so that I wound up with my gaze on an attractive woman in an expensively tailored suit. The glance she gave me clearly communicated that she felt I was a big fat loser for not conducting international business while standing in line.

Thank goodness I even had a cell phone. I pulled it out and frowned at it importantly. "I can't believe I haven't head from them," I fumed out loud. I punched in a number, met the businesswoman's eyes, and sighed. "Berlin office," I explained. "Just because they're four hours ahead, they think they can stop working."

"Actually, I think they're nine hours ahead," she responded.

"Right, that's true in most of Berlin," I nodded sagely. Fortunately, the person who answered the phone at my department at the newspaper was my friend Sarah, who I figured I could pull into my plan without her having the slightest idea what was going on.

"I'm calling about our merger. I'm really interested in obtaining some more of that accidental petroleum," I boomed.

"I can already tell that *this* is going to be an interesting conversation," Sarah answered. "Do go on."

"Er . . . I don't care if you are four hours ahead, the rest of Berlin is nine hours ahead, so you'd think you'd be grateful for that," I informed her.

"Aren't you at the airport? Wait, let me guess. All the other men are having business calls on their cell phones, so you're feeling less masculine," she observed, leading me to believe she was close to figuring out my clever ploy.

"Of course not! I have as much steel cable as anyone," I stated archly.

"I can't believe you would compete over something so silly as the importance of your cell phone call. Thank God as men get older they run out of testosterone—maybe in a few years you'll stop acting so crazy," she reproved. "It's nature's way of remodeling a man."

"Thanks for the update." I hung up and stared thoughtfully at the telephone. I wondered if what she had said were true, that as I got older I might have less testosterone and need shots or something to keep up with everyone else.

Was it crazy to pretend to be talking about international business deals with Sarah? Or did it make perfect sense? I glanced again at the woman behind me, and decided to get her opinion.

"I'm sorry, but I have to ask you something. Did you by chance happen to overhear any of my conversation?"

"Yes. I'm sorry. I wasn't eavesdropping, but you were talking rather loudly," she responded.

I nodded. So it did make perfect sense! I *was* as big and important as the accidental cable installers. "Okay, thanks," I told her.

COMPETITIVENESS IS HARD-WIRED INTO US— YOU DO UNDERSTAND WHY MEN LIKE THE IDEA OF BEING "HARD-WIRED," DON'T YOU?

Look, aren't there times when people are supposed to compete? Recently my sister the doctor challenged me to a board game in which the contestants advance their positions by correctly answering trivial questions off small cards. This is a competitive situation, right? Yet, as I think you'll see, my sister reacted churlishly to the whole thing when I began to outscore her.

"Okay, first question," she announced. She held up the card. "When adrift at sea, how can you determine when you are close to land?"

"You see the shore," I answered promptly.

"That's not one of the choices," she told me.

"But it's the obvious answer, don't you think?"

"You're too far away to see the shore in this."

"Does it say that?" I challenged.

"No, but it's implied in the question. Look, let me just read the answers to you," she said impatiently.

See how she was getting competitive already?

"A: You see land-based birds in the air; B: You see muddy water and surface debris such as sticks; C: The wind changes direction in the evening; or D: The swells define themselves into choppier waves."

"Obviously A," I stated.

"No, you're wrong. It's B." She reached out and moved her game piece forward.

I cocked my head. "Well, actually, if you think about it, if you see land-based birds, it pretty much means they are coming from land, right? Otherwise they wouldn't think of themselves as 'land-based.' So I'm going to have to allow that one as well."

"What? You can't 'allow' something. The answer is B."

"Sorry, but I'm just being logical," I countered logically.

"It's not the right answer!"

"See, this is why you had trouble in school," I advised her kindly. "You always took things at face value."

"What do you mean, had trouble in school?"

"I had to help you with your homework all the time."

"What? I helped *you*. Don't you remember that we would sit at the kitchen table and you'd say, 'Just tell me the answers'?" she stormed.

"I wanted you to tell me the answers so you'd learn how to do the homework," I said primly. "Anyway, I always took more challenging classes. Same with college," I pointed out.

"Are you kidding? I was biology major, and you were an English major."

"Sorry, but have you even read *Moby Dick*? In biology class, the elbow is always attached to the wrist, but in the world of literature, everything is open to interpretation."

"The elbow isn't . . . of course I read . . . I wrote a paper on *Moby Dick*!"

I took my sister's stuttering as evidence that she'd had enough, and elected to let the matter drop, particularly since she stood up with a disgusted noise and stomped from the room.

From this event, one can draw several conclusions. First, that my sister is as competitive as I, perhaps even more so. Her refusal to allow me to advance my game piece when I clearly had the correct answer shows how far she was willing to go to prevent me from winning. Second, it's pretty obvious she's still trying to compete with me for grades, long after we've both graduated. Why else would she have brought it up? And finally, obviously an English major is far more challenging than a biology program—there are a lot fewer books written about biology than there are in English, after all.

We can conclude, then, this is another instance where the behavior of the male of the species is the direct result of the actions of my sister. Were she not so belligerent, I would not have felt as if we were competing, and would not have felt compelled to defeat her in the debate.

So there's one way to keep men from being competitive: Stop trying to compete with them.

As a Changed Man, I am willing to go further and relate an incident that reveals an even more effective way to disarm the competitive response in men. I call it That One Time When I Was Forced to End a Competition with My Neighbor Even Though I Was Winning.

THAT ONE TIME WHEN I WAS FORCED TO END A COMPETITION WITH MY NEIGHBOR EVEN THOUGH I WAS WINNING

One fall I was sitting on my couch watching my favorite landscape artist, God, fill my lawn full of leaves. Now, my position on yard work as always been "What God has joined together let no man rake up," so I was perfectly content to allow the trees to shed their colorful load. Then my neighbor Tom walked out into his yard with what looked like a vacuum cleaner. Trailing a long extension cord, he strode up to the property line between our two homes, aiming his device at a small pile of leaves. With a buzzing noise, his appliance stirred them up, and they danced out ahead of Tom.

Right into my yard.

"Whatcha got there, a leaf blower?" I asked when I trotted up to Tom.

He nodded proudly. "It's an E-1000. Just bought it." He swept the nozzle in a wide semicircle, the leaves moving ahead of him like advancing soldiers invading my country and making off with my women.

"Pretty cool," I observed. "Mind if I give it a try?"

Tom bit his lip. "Well, I don't know. The thing is, it is pretty complicated. The manual is almost thirty pages long."

"You read the manual?" I jeered.

"No, of course not," he replied hurriedly. "But I just thought I shouldn't let any of my neighbors use it before I checked with the manual to see if it was okay, is all."

"Tom, we're not just neighbors. We're best friends, right? I mean, if I had a leaf thrower, you know I'd let you use it."

"Leaf *blower.*"

"Whatever. The point is, that's the kind of friends we are, am I right?"

He shrugged. "Well, you wouldn't let me use your Shop-Vac," he pointed out.

"Right, Shop-*Vac*," I agreed impatiently. "But a leaf *blower* is different, don't you think?"

I had him there. With a sigh, he slipped the strap off his shoulder and handed the thing over. It was a little awkward at first, because the rear-mounted motor made the thing tip up, but I do think Tom overreacted when the blast of dirty air hit him in the face. I mean, who *doesn't* get dirt in his eyes when doing yard work?

After about twenty minutes, I'd moved ten square yards of leaves into Tom's yard. I handed him the blower with a sweet smile. "Thanks, that was fun!" I told him. He nodded, his face troubled. He'd gotten the message.

Later that afternoon I happened to glance out my window, and I froze in shock. Not only had Tom been out working in his yard some more, but he had blown nearly three quarters of his yard into mine! I would never have suspected Tom of such treachery, because normally about half an hour of weekend chores is all he can tolerate.

I was at the hardware store within fifteen minutes, explaining my dilemma to Sam, the guy who owns the place. He's about seventy years old and never leaves the store. I think at night he sleeps in a crate of bolts. His face crinkled thoughtfully as I explained what a horrible person Tom had become.

"An E-1000, eh?" Sam mused. "That's a nice unit."

"Well it's turned Tom into some sort of raving lunatic. I'm worried that I might have to go over to his house and cut down all of his trees or something, just to insert some sanity into this thing."

"I am having a sale on chainsaws," Sam agreed thoughtfully. "But I wonder if perhaps you wouldn't be better off fighting fire with fire."

"I could burn his trees!" I enthused.

Sam shook his head. "Nope, I was thinking more like the E-3000." Sam reached up onto the rack and pulled down a gleaming monster of a leaf blower, the electric motor larger than a basketball. "Most powerful electric I've got. Nozzle blast the equivalent of a fire hose. Superior technology. You could probably drive a windmill at a hundred yards with this baby."

"I'll take it. Does it have any attachments that shoot projectiles?"

The manual for the E-3000 had a lot of really important warnings, which I figured I would read if I ever had time. Once I got home I strode out into my yard, lugging my new toy over my shoulder. I saw Tom watching pensively from his front window. The electric cord, thick as a high tension wire, snaked behind me.

I aimed my blower at a particularly offensive pile of leaves and pulled the trigger. Instantly the air was torn by the thunderous roar of an angry E-3000. Dirt and leaves swirled in front of me, a maelstrom that caused small pieces of gravel to bounce audibly off the side of Tom's house.

When I released the trigger and looked at my handiwork, the grass had all been flattened like an alien crop circle, and the leaves were gone.

Tom came out to talk to me. "Hey."

"Oh hi Tom!" I responded cheerfully. "I was just out here using the most powerful electric leaf blower known to the history of mankind."

"An E-3000," he noted. "Pretty nice."

"Thanks!"

"But you're sort of blowing leaves into my yard."

"Oh. Well, right, but only the leaves that you blew into my yard in the first place," I responded.

"That's ridiculous. How do you know which is which?"

I patted the motor on the E-3000. "Superior technology."

"Ah. Well . . . Mind if I try her out?"

I shook my head. "Sorry Tom, but this one has a manual more than a hundred pages long."

He watched me for a few more minutes, then turned and went back inside his house, where he probably crawled into the fetal position.

The next morning I was awakened by an odd buzzing noise. I went to the window, expecting to see a large bee carrying off the neighborhood children. Instead, I witnessed something horrible: Tom was out in his yard, blasting leaves with a diabolical device.

"Morning Tom!" I yelled at him. He flicked a switch and the noise died. "Whatcha got, there?"

"A G-3000," he said proudly. "The 'G' stands for 'gas-driven.' It's the most powerful leaf blower on the market. You should see the manual for *this* baby!"

"Why would you buy a gas-powered blower? That's fossil fuel technology, don't you care about the environment?"

He shook his head. "Nope."

"What kind of person doesn't care about the environment?" I demanded, outraged.

"The kind of person's got a G-3000 twice as powerful as yours," he answered snidely.

We stood for a minute, regarding each other from our respective properties. "I wouldn't blow your leaves in my yard anymore, Tom," I warned quietly.

He smiled. "Yeah? What are you going to do, use your electric leaf blower and send them back? Because if you do"—he patted the motor on his G-3000—"the two of us can handle it."

He went back to his satanic yard work. When I got to the hardware store, Sam was sympathetic, but unhelpful.

"Sorry, Bruce," he clucked, "but Tom got the last of the G-3000s. I can sell you a G-2000, though. Pretty powerful."

"Sam, you have to help me, here," I pleaded. "A G-2000 is no good. I have to be able to out-blow a G-3000."

Sam's craggy face turned dark and troubled. He bit his lip. "Well . . . there is one thing . . ."

"What? What is it, Sam?" I cried.

He shrugged. "Factory rep brought me a Jet G-5000 X series leaf blower to try out."

"I'll take it!" I cried.

He held up his hand. "Hang on, Bruce. I can't legally sell it to you. The EPA has issued a ban. They have to be fitted with a special exhaust filter, and I don't have those in yet. The way it is now, it would be pretty bad for the environment."

"I don't care about that, Sam. Now, you and I are both Americans, am I right? We have to stick together on this."

"Isn't Tom an American?"

I waved my hand. "I'm only saying, Sam, there are times when a man has to stand up and do what is right, and there are times when he doesn't, and this is one of those times. Am I right?"

"I . . . what?"

"How much for the X series, Sam? Name your price."

I nearly fainted, but my hands were trembling with determination when I gave Sam my credit card. I pictured the women at the bank, glancing at each other as they approved the purchase. "He's buying an X series," they'd whisper. "What a man."

I could barely lift the thing out of the car, and my back was bowed with the weight of it as I staggered to my property line. I flipped the safety switches, then watched as the countdown ticked off on the starter display. At T minus-three seconds the engine began to whine, and I planted my feet. Tom came out of his house to see what I was up to.

At ignition there was a roar like an atomic blast. I staggered backward, pushed around in circles by the sheer force of the Jet G-5000. The noise was deafening, and so much dust filled the air I couldn't see anything. Choking, I fumbled for the emergency kill switch.

The stillness that followed was almost ethereal. All the birds had fallen silent, and a furrow like that of a horse-drawn plow was cut into the earth where I had aimed the business end of the Jet G-5000.

Tom slowly got to his feet, mystified that he was missing his shirt and shoes. He limped over to me, and I crawled out from under the weight of the Jet G-5000 and stood up.

"You okay?" he asked hoarsely.

I nodded. "I think so."

We stood silently for a moment, staring down at the muscled contours of the Jet G-5000. Tom spat some dirt from his mouth. "I have to get me one of those," he said.

Now, there are several lessons to be learned from this leaf-blowing story, the most important being, I won. However, this incident led to another advancement in my understanding of what it's like to be a Changed Man: Tom's wife Emily had watched this drama unfold all weekend, and, probably smarting from the defeat of her husband, decided to intervene. I had finished leaf blowing and was reading on the sofa when Emily knocked on my door, waking me up.

"Well, we won," she stated, as soon as I opened the door.

I blinked at her. "Won what?"

She pointed out into her yard. "I had the Brownie troop over, and they raked our yard. All the leaves are up. So we won."

I leaned out and looked. Her yard was, indeed, immaculate. And I have to confess that, though it was the most powerful leaf blower on the market, the Jet G-5000 didn't actually do a very good job of getting leaves off the lawn. But to say Emily had "won" was silly, and I told her so.

"Well, we decided to see if the girls could do a better job, and they did," Emily responded after I finished explaining about the Jet G-5000's horsepower rating. "So we won."

I stepped outside. "There's a leaf," I pointed out smugly. An oak tree in the middle of her property had released a brown and curled leaf, which fluttered to the ground before our eyes.

"Yes, but you have lots of leaves in your yard," Emily replied.

"So?" I responded testily.

Emily shrugged, turning to depart. "Well, just thought you'd like to know that you lost."

"I did not lose!"

Emily stopped on the bottom step and squinted up at me, and then uttered the words that made me a Changed Man forever when it came to competition: "The girls are still at my house. They'll rake your yard for ten dollars."

I've always believed in supporting organizations like the Brownies, and besides once they had raked my yard it was completely leaf-free, so I did win after all.

I returned the Jet G-5000 to Sam, who took it back in with his customary 10 percent restocking fee, so I was only out four hundred dollars. I figured it was worth it, because of the valuable lesson I learned that day about myself and about the raking abilities of Brownies.

TIP So there's the lesson for anyone who wants to remodel a man's competitive nature: Redefine the contest so that he has a choice between winning or losing to a bunch of girls. He'll pick winning every time.

FIGHTING THE MOTHER
OF ALL NATURES

To understand why men are so competitive, you must look to a time before they were men, or even boys. Your examination should go all the way back to the moment of his conception, which I admit is a little difficult to do if you are already dating him.

What I know about human reproduction I learned in my fifth-grade sex education class. We watched a cartoon that depicted a long-tailed fellow named Herm whose focus in life was to swim upstream as fast as he could, beating out hundreds of other cartoon swimmers in order to be able to literally collide with Megg, his true love. Megg was sort of round, with big puffy lips and long eyelashes—it was a bit difficult to see what Herm found so attractive, but he seemed sincere in his affections.

As Herm explained it, he and his buddies spent most of their time pushing and shoving each other good-naturedly, waiting for the starting pistol to go off. Then it was all one big race—in other words, a competition.

Naturally, my classmates and I were completely baffled by this movie, which fell far short of explaining what we were hoping to find out in this class: how to get a girlfriend. I remember discussing the matter with my pals out on the playground at recess, eventually concluding that if the situation ever came up, Brad Smith would probably be the one who became a father because he always won the fifty-yard dash in gym class.

My friend Drake contended he would win because he had a three-speed, but we doubted that when the time came they would let you ride your bicycle.

That Herm's sole reason for existing was so he could participate in a race wasn't even discussed. For boys, the idea that life itself is nothing more than a giant competition doesn't seem anything but natural.

Here's the lesson of this chapter: Just because men compete, it doesn't mean we like it. We do it because we have to, because we are as compelled and single-minded as Herm and the rest of the members of the swim team. We'd prefer not to have to bother going down to the hardware store for a new leaf blower, but it's wired into our nature because we want to win.

And by "win" I mean, of course, "not lose"—particularly if it is to a Brownie troop.

The lesson of the leaf-blower incident, That One Time When I Was Forced to End a Competition with My Neighbor Even Though I Was Winning, is that men will compete not to lose, but if they are certain to lose, they will try not to compete. I'm enough of a Changed Man to recognize that when it comes to raking leaves, a Brownie troop is superior technology.

A final way to remodel a man when it comes to competition is to identify a disqualifying factor—that is, a reason why the contest is so unfair the man can, with considerable relief, opt out.

TIP ⟩ Try this sometime:

HIM:

I can't believe Hurly bought a brand-new Ford Explorer! (Meaning: *Now I have to get a Lincoln Navigator.*)

YOU:

Oh, he didn't buy it, he leased it. (Meaning: *He's cheating!*)

Of course, you can always use a man's nature for the reverse effect.

YOU:

Look at Hurly out there, taking down his Christmas decorations. He's going to beat you again this year! (Meaning: *It would be nice for once if we didn't still have a plastic Santa in the yard on Memorial Day.*)

HIM:

Oh no, he's not going to beat me! (Meaning: *I am a dumb male who is easily manipulated!*)

These two tactics: (a) demonstrating to a man that he is doomed to lose, or (b) pointing out that the other side must be cheating, are equally effective. Either way, you'll dull a man's competitive edge—plus your yard will probably get raked in the process.

7.

\- \- \-

COMMUNICATION

How to Contact the Male
Brain via the Ears

When talking to each other, men fall into a hierarchical pattern I call Mr. Communicating. When talking to women, they use Ms. Communicating. At the center of every conversation a man has with a woman is Ms. Communication.

Men receive and process information differently than women. Take, for example, those advertisements for automobile parts that run in car magazines. They'll show a beautiful blonde in a bikini holding a muffler and grinning as if standing around clutching car parts is a much better alternative than going to the beach. Men see this and conclude: *Maybe if I buy that kind of muffler, women in bikinis will be hanging all over me.* Women see the ad and conclude: *Men are idiots.*

When you ask us a question, we are less likely to route it through our logic circuits than to react like this:

Male Communication Process

THOUGHT TREE

Question: "What do you think?"

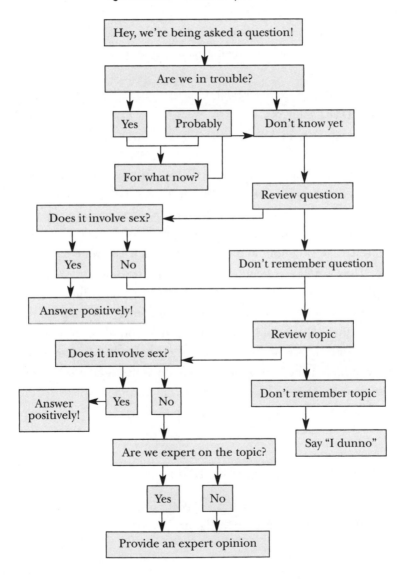

The above allows us to draw several conclusions:

1. Mapping the male brain is similar to mapping Wyoming: A few little points of activity with lots of space in between.
2. Often you think men aren't listening, but actually they're just not paying attention.
3. Though a man may know nothing about a topic, he nonetheless believes he knows more about it than you do.

THE DIFFERENCES SHOW UP EARLY

As a Changed Man, I can advise you I've observed that males and females are drawn to discuss different topics. Women seem interested in feelings, ideas, and emotions. Men seem interested in themselves. Women make their points in a conversation by using references to situations and events with which everyone can identify. "How would you like it," they will ask, "if something like that happened to you?" Men make their points by talking more loudly than the person with whom they are disagreeing. "How would you like it," they will ask, "if I punched you in the nose?"

The differences in the way the sexes communicate show up early in life. My nephew is eight years old, and I recently scientifically observed him at play with two slightly younger girls who were pretending to be princesses planning a tea party.

PRINCESS #1:

We'll invite everyone from the land.

PRINCESS #2:

(holding a bear) This is Baby Henry. He was very sick.

NEPHEW:

I'm bored.

PRINCESS #1:

Poor Baby Henry. Let's set him here at the head of the table.

PRINCESS #2:

Everyone is so glad to see him!

PRINCESS #1:

(holding a female doll, speaking in a falsetto) Hello Henry. You look so handsome.

NEPHEW:

Can we just start playing now?

PRINCESS #2:

(on behalf of Henry) Thank you, Princess Leah.

PRINCESS #1:

Would you like to come to the party?

PRINCESS #2:

Yes I would.

PRINCESS #1:

You can sit next to me at the head of the table.

NEPHEW:

We already said that! (Falls on grass and looks heavenward with a take-me-now-Lord expression on his face.)

PRINCESS #2:

Let's say Baby Henry is really the prince but he doesn't know it.

PRINCESS #1:

Well, but then he can't marry Princess Leah.

NEPHEW:

That's *Star Wars* and in *Star Wars* she doesn't marry a bear!

PRINCESS #2:

Let's say they are from different kingdoms.

PRINCESS #1:

Yes!

NEPHEW:

I'll be the king. (standing) I declare war on you, Princess Leah.

PRINCESS #2:

No, because Baby Henry is engaged to Princess Leah, they are doing peace now.

NEPHEW:

Why are we playing this stupid game?

PRINCESS #1:

And everyone was happy when they found out Baby Henry was the prince!

NEPHEW:

(falls over with a groan)

Clearly, though these girls are just children, they've already begun to display signs of not understanding that the king always has the power to declare war. The princesses happily chattered on and on, while my nephew waited with increasing impatience for an actual game to commence. As far as he was concerned, they could have dispensed with conversation altogether, and just gone straight to the sword fight.

A MALE'S VERBAL SKILLS
ARE SLOW TO DEVELOP,
AND THEN THEY STOP

This preference for action over words only intensifies as boys grow older. As they reach their teen years, their brains become drenched in testosterone—a hormone that is rich in nutrients like anger and stupidity—and they develop a style of communication geared toward the social skills of obnoxiousness and repugnance. Their sullen swagger comes out in a verbal strut, a way of saying, "Watch it baby, you don't want to mess with me, I'm a hundred-and-two pounds of pure man."

When I was in high school, I became overly impressed with my friend Randy, who confided the following:

"When I get home from school and I want to go out, man, I don't tell my parents nothing. They go, 'Randy where are you going?' and I go 'Out,' and they go 'What do you mean, out?' and I don't say nothing else, man, I just walk out that door."

I decided to use this same tough, taciturn method of communicating with my own parents. That Friday night, I went to the mirror and sneered at it a little, preparing myself for the lack of conversation to come. Randy had a tough way of walking, a subtle swagger I couldn't emulate without making it look like I had hip dysplasia, but I found I could adopt Randy's laconic scowl without too much difficulty.

The plan was for Randy to come over and pick me up at the foot of the driveway. The two of us would cruise around with sullen faces, looking so fierce the cops would glance at each other in concern when they saw us, calling in the license plate number of the car we were driving—Randy's mother's station wagon—to make sure there were no outstanding warrants for felony intimidation.

At the appointed hour, I walked down the stairs and right past my parents, who were watching television. When I got to the front door, I peeked over my shoulder to see if they were gaping at this masculine apparition that had just stalked through the living room.

They didn't even look up.

Frowning, I went back through the living room and into the kitchen. I slammed down a glass of milk like a cowboy taking a hit of whiskey, wiping my mouth with the back of my wrist. Okay, time to roll out Randy's walk. I strutted into the living room, making sure I broke their gaze on the TV screen by arrogantly strolling right in front of it.

This time they did notice. "What's the matter, honey, did you stub your toe?" my mother asked solicitously.

I was at the front door again, and they still hadn't asked me where I was going. I put my hand on the knob and glanced over at her, but their attention was back on the TV screen. "I'm leaving," I snarled pointedly. "I don't know what time I'll be back."

This gained my father's interest at last. "Where are you going?" he demanded.

Perfect.

"Out," I pronounced, not bothering to glance over my shoulder to see them flinch at my brutality.

I didn't say nothin' else, man, I just walked out that door and strode to the end of the driveway. Randy would be by any minute. I stood insolently at the curb, my posture indicating that I was the sort of person who should be avoided. Old Mrs. Martin cruised by in her big Buick, and I spat contemptuously in the street. She waved gaily.

I swiveled to look back at the house. Both of my parents were standing in the big picture window, gazing with what I assumed was no small amount of dread at their transformed son. My mother turned, and in the light from the lamp I could clearly read her lips as she asked my father, "What is he doing out there?"

A few minutes later I heard my dad leave the house. He came and stood next to me in the darkness of the evening. "It cost me two dollars," he advised.

My cold stare faltered a little. I couldn't help but ask, "What did?"

"The stencil." He pointed to the curb, which had our street address freshly painted on it in reflective material. I hadn't noticed. "That's what you're looking at, isn't it?"

I'd been out there at the end of the driveway for fifteen minutes and my father thought my attention was riveted by some numbers stenciled on the cement?

"Anyway." He clapped me on the shoulder. "Somebody named Randy called for you. He said he can't come over tonight, he's grounded."

WE DON'T GROW OUT OF IT

Eventually, men emerge from adolescence—or so I've been told, anyway. Yet we still want to be seen as tough and laconic, and we're still impatient with any conversational details that don't directly describe action and instead dwell on such extraneous elements as character and emotions.

My friend Tom struggles with this all the time. We recently went to see a movie together because his wife, Emily, wasn't interested in the plot, which involved blowing up a lot of machinery and people. When we got back to Tom's place, Emily was still up.

"How was the movie?" she asked her husband.

"Fine."

"What was it about?" she wanted to know. This was a bit bewildering to Tom, because the advertisement in the newspaper clearly showed explosions, tanks, and dying.

Tom shrugged uncomfortably. "The war."

"I mean, what was the plot, what happened?"

Tom looked baffled. "In the war? We won," he said.

Emily seemed to think this was an insufficient report. Yet for all of her thirst for details, she was completely furious when a few nights later, at a party, Tom called from across the room, "Hey Emily, didn't you say you're up to a hundred and fifty-five pounds?"

Apparently sometimes women want more details, and sometimes they want less. Men just have to guess.

HOW I'VE CHANGED:
BRUCE THE ANSWER MAN

As you can see from the succinct analysis above, I've become very sensitive to the different ways men and women communicate. My sister the teacher says, "Men talk as if everything is all about them, like they're the most important thing on earth." Well, it's not that simple, which is why I was so pleased to be able to discuss the topic of men and communications on a local radio station's talk show.*

The host, Jim, seated me next to a woman my age, a Professor Salazar, and spoke into the microphone.

"We're lucky to have with us Dr. Patricia Salazar, professor of anthropology at the University of California. Professor Salazar is author of *Gender Differences in Communication: A Comprehensive Analysis of Vagaries in Human Speech Patterns Throughout the World.* Dr. Salazar also holds a Ph.D. in biology, she was recently voted one of the ten most important women in the world by *Human Intelligencia* maga-

---

*I'm actually something of a veteran broadcaster, having once been on the air with a local AM talk show during the popular "Saturday at noon" radio listening hour. It was eventually canceled because, in the words of the station manager, it was "a call-in show with no callers and a humor show with no humor."

zine, and, Dr. Salazar, you're also a painter with an art exhibit opening at the Whitney next week, isn't that right?"

She nodded. "That's right."

"Well welcome, Doctor, and congratulations, by the way, on the Congressional Award. We also have nationally syndicated humor columnist W. Bruce Cameron." He frowned at his notes. "Mr. Cameron, you've written a book . . ."

"Writing a book," I corrected.

"Writing a book on . . . remodeling?" He turned and looked through the glass at his producer, who shrugged helplessly.

"I was also social chairman of my fraternity," I stated.

"I see. Well, Dr. Salazar, suppose we start with you. What would you say is a key difference between the way men communicate and the way women do?"

She steepled her fingers. "Well, Jim, that's an interesting question."

"I agree," I agreed. "Very interesting. Men are much more direct in their conversations, much more about getting to the point, without a lot of side-tracking. Of course, it's different now with e-mail, which I feel has really changed things. You can really get distracted with that stuff. I get a couple of dozen e-mails a day, most of them about Viagra. Which I don't need! I mean, I don't ask for these, they just show up in my mailbox. I'm thinking of getting a new computer. I might even switch from Windows to Mac."

There was a pause. Jim turned back to the woman. "You were saying, Dr. Salazar?"

"I was just going to say, men are much more likely to interrupt and state their opinions, even if they are ill-informed and off-topic."

They both looked at me. "Okay, ha," I said.

The doctor leaned forward into the microphone. "For men, conversation is about status. They use discussion to establish who is in control. The pecking order, if you will. To a man, it is important to determine the hierarchy."

"I believe I had the floor," I pointed out.

"Women are listeners," Dr. Salabaster continued. "They participate in conversations in order to establish relationships, and one of the ways they do this is to demonstrate their concern for the other person by actively listening. It shows they care. Men are talkers. Listening isn't as important to them, unless they are listening to themselves."

Jim turned to me. "Mr. Cameron?"

"Yes?"

"Your response?"

"Huh?"

"Your response to what Dr. Salazar just said?"

"Oh. Well . . . I think one thing that men do is that we're very informative. We give good information when we talk."

"Such as?" he prodded.

"Excuse me?"

"What sort of information?"

"Oh, you know." I shrugged. "Facts."

Jim apparently felt I was getting too technical, so he turned back to Dr. Salamander.

"What else can you tell us, Dr. Salazar?"

"Well," she mused, "women care much more about the details than men do. They are much more interested in what someone was wearing, for example . . . To them, saying you saw someone interesting in a restaurant may be the point of the story, but they are also interested in hearing about which restaurant, what you had to eat, and, of course, whether you had dessert. Men just want a report on what happened, and they get dismissive when you provide too much of what they consider to be extraneous detail."

"Mr. Cameron?"

I waved a hand. "Whatever."

At commercial break, the producer came in, shook my hand, and thanked me for coming. I noted somewhat smugly that Dr. Saladlicker was asked to stay for the next segment—apparently she had done such a poor job explaining her position they felt it necessary to hold on to her for additional elucidation.

REMODELING A MAN WHO WON'T ASK FOR DIRECTIONS

Let's move from the general observation that men and women communicate differently to the more specific question of how to remodel a man so that he'll communicate in a fashion that is less exasperating. In the thousands of letters I have received regarding male behavior, one criticism emerges above all others when it comes to communications: Men Who Won't Ask for Directions.

Now, much has been said and written about the unfortunate tendency of women to ask for directions from complete strangers who cannot possibly know where we are going. Men seem to understand much better than women that all roads lead somewhere—if you just keep driving, eventually you're bound to wind up at a destination.*

TIP ⟩ If this is an issue in your own relationship, you may want to consider the method my friend Sarah utilized to turn me into a Changed Man on the topic. I was driving her to an office party. Her boyfriend Doug wasn't going, and "Don't ask" was the reason she gave me. We were running late when it became apparent to me that we were taking an alternative route—in other words, we were lost. I was focused on becoming found, with Sarah sitting next to me providing me with unhelpful observations like, "That's the sec-

---

*This can be verified with a simple experiment. Get in your car, and drive in any direction at random for any period of time. At some point, pull over, park, and get out of the car. Look around. See? You've arrived *somewhere*. Even though you didn't have any idea where you were going, you got there with no problem. This is something men grasp intuitively, but which women seem to have a hard time understanding.

ond time we've passed that gas station. Are you sure you know where you are going?"

This was a silly question. I could look out the windshield and see where we were going. It was the party whose location was a mystery. "I think maybe I need to head north."

"I thought you said we were heading north."

I frowned at her. Sarah might be the smartest woman I know, always quick to help me come up with an excuse to tell my editor why my column is late, but there was a downside to Sarah's intellect: She seemed awfully quick to point out whenever she thought I might be making a mistake. Men hate this. They are cognitive learners who want to be able to experience and grow on their own so that they can be free to ignore their errors. "You're not helping, Sarah."

"Sorry."

We drove on in silence for a few moments. I made a number of turns, my confidence growing that I had us back on the right track. Then Sarah mumbled something.

"What?" I asked her.

"I just said, 'There's the gas station again.'"

"Look, do you want to drive?" I asked irritably.

"Sure!" she agreed brightly.

"Well, then please stop pointing out gas stations. I don't need gas."

"There's a police station, we could stop there," she suggested impractically.

I moodily ignored this. A manly man certainly doesn't ask directions from people with guns.

She was quiet for a few minutes. "Say, see that man over there?"

I glanced out the window at a gentleman standing on the corner.

"He looks lost," she continued. "Could we pull over and help him?"

I thought this sounded very charitable, and drove up to the

corner, rolling down my window. "Hey there, you lost?" I hailed him.

He frowned. "I've lived here all my life."

Sarah leaned over. "We're on our way to the MacDonnells' party, and thought if you were going there too we could give you directions."

"The MacDonnells? They live just three blocks up, take a left at the gas station, then left again at the first stop sign. It's kind of tricky, you have to be careful you don't wind up driving in a big circle."

I smiled. "Well, that doesn't sound right, but if you don't want our help, so be it." I rolled up my window and left the guy standing there.

"See? If we followed his instructions we'd be lost for days," I pointed out.

"Let's do what he suggested, just to prove how wrong he was," Sarah agreed.

This seemed reasonable. We turned and then by accident spotted the MacDonnells' house. "Well, what do you know," I murmured. I shot a triumphant look at my friend. "Seems like just relaxing about it and letting me drive got us here in no time at all."

She nodded. "It sure looks that way."

Because Sarah is smarter than I, she was able to remodel me so that no woman has ever since complained about my driving whenever it appears, however erroneously, that I might have made a wrong turn. If I feel like I have taken an alternative route, I will make a point of looking for people who are wandering around lost, and pull over and give them help. Often during the course of instructing these individuals on where they should be going, I figure out the proper route for my own travels. Apparently the old adage that "The best way to learn is to teach" is especially apt when it comes to finding directions.

WHEN THE Y CHROMOSOME GETS LODGED IN THE EAR CANAL

As an Expert in How the Sexes Communicate, I've discovered why women feel men aren't listening to them. Men, you see, talk in turn. Each man says his piece, with all the other men being relatively silent, and then the next man talks. Women are much more interactive, interjecting each other's conversations with comments.

With this realization, I have remodeled myself to communicate more effectively with women. Here's how my interactions used to go:

WOMAN:

My friend Belinda is feeling so blue. Her cat was sick, you know, and she took him in and it turns out he has some sort of skin infection and she has to hold him down and give him injections every day. The poor little thing, they don't understand, you know, and she says it just breaks her heart to have to do it to him, and now he runs from her when she walks in the door! She says it is like her best friend in the world is afraid of her. And then there's her boyfriend Rob, he got laid off again, and he doesn't know what he's going to do and Belinda is just worried sick. It seems like everything is going wrong with her right now. So we're thinking of maybe having a little get together tonight after work, sort of try to cheer her up. What do you think?

FORMER ME:

Huh?

WOMAN:

You heartless bastard!

And here is how I interact now, providing meaningful feedback that communicates the message, "I am listening to you."

WOMAN:

My friend Belinda is feeling so blue.

CHANGED ME:

Belinda?

WOMAN:

Her cat was sick, you know, and she took him in and it turns out he has some sort of skin infection . . .

CHANGED ME:

Her cat was sick?

WOMAN:

Right, and she has to hold him down and give him injections every day.

CHANGED ME:

Injections?

WOMAN:

Yes! The poor little thing, they don't understand, you know.

CHANGED ME:

They don't understand.

WOMAN:

Um, right, and she says it just breaks her heart to have to do it to him, and now he runs from her when she walks in the door!

CHANGED ME:

She breaks her door.

WOMAN:

What? No, it breaks her heart.

CHANGED ME:

It breaks her heart when she walks in the door.

WOMAN:

Right, because of her cat!

CHANGED ME:

It breaks her heart when the cat walks in the door.

WOMAN:

You heartless bastard!

Well, perhaps I still need some work on this whole process, but you get the idea of what I am attempting. I'm a Changed Man—most men require substantial remodeling to attain this level of empathy in their conversations.

There are times, though, when all you want is for your man to just listen to you—for example, when you're speaking. Men have selective hearing in their conversations, and the default selection is "off." To change a man, you need to sprinkle your dialogue with little verbal tidbits to force him to leave his hearing "on," like this:

WOMAN:

My friend Belinda is feeling so blue. Her cat was sick, you know, and she had bare breasts, so she took him in and it turns out he has some sort of skin infection and she has to take her clothes off and give him injections every day. The poor little thing, they don't understand, you know, nudity, and she says it just breaks her heart to have to do it to him, and now he runs from her when she walks in the door wearing lingerie! And then she has sex with her boyfriend Rob, he got laid off again, and he doesn't know what he's going to do and Belinda is just worried naked. It seems like everything is going wrong with her right now. So we're thinking of maybe having a little get together tonight after work, bra and panties, sort of try to cheer her up. What do you think?

Of course, we've already covered this: He doesn't think. But you've certainly got his attention!

GIVE HIM SOMETHING TO CROW ABOUT

At the risk of agreeing with my radio friend Dr. Salivater, I do believe men see a conversation as something of a contest, using words to establish the pecking order the way male dogs mark bushes and trees. (I think we can all agree that the human method is more socially pleasing than the other one.) Men believe that the primary purpose of talking is to communicate information, and that information is, "I'm important."

Remember, to a man, his world is a hen house, and he's the rooster. He wants to stand on the roof and shout, "There's the sun! I invented it! I'm in charge of making it rise!" Your job is to resist the temptation to shove him off the roof. It won't do you any good to try to explain to him that he's less important than he thinks—all that will gain you is a morose rooster.

Instead, look to someone like me for hope. As a Changed Man, my conversational skills have improved to the point that when I am in a group of people, I rank as the top communicator! Gentle, positive reinforcement will overcome his natural maleness and the residual effects of testosterone, eventually enabling him to be much better at talking and listening without turning it into some sort of competition, though he probably won't be as good at it as I am.

Of course, trying to have a deep conversation with a man is a bit like attempting to scuba dive in the baby pool. Just because you can get him to sit up and pay attention to you in hopes of encountering another reference to naked Belinda doesn't mean you'll find what he has to say any more interesting than it was before. If you want to remodel his topics, see chapter fourteen, which offers some advanced tips on the difficult task of changing his very nature.

8.

\- \- \-

THE 200-POUND BABY

All Men Are Secondhand— You Get Them from Their Mommies

Take a man to the natural history museum and show him a diorama of daily life for the Cro-Magnons, and he'll nod approvingly. "Yep," he'll comment, "that's what it was like. The men are off with their spears hunting ferocious beasts, and the women are at home doing the easy work." Never mind that the Cro-Magnons were alive forty thousand years ago and that it's pretty hard to tell from somebody's *bones* who had the "easier job." A man enjoys the Cro-Magnon display because that's sort of the way he wishes it were now—that he and his friends could spend the day stalking what is essentially a big cow while their wives did all the rest of the work.

CRO-MAGNON MAN:

Lucy, I'm home!

CRO-MAGNON WOMAN:

Hello dear, how did your day go?

CRO-MAGNON MAN:

Fine, how was yours?

CRO-MAGNON WOMAN:

Oh, fine. First I had to fend off a pack of wolves that were after the children. Then I butchered the bison you brought home yesterday. I hung the skin to dry and cooked the meat. I went into the fields and gathered some fruit. I hauled the ashes out of the fire pit, and brought water from the river. Then I had a baby.

CRO-MAGNON MAN:

I wish I had such an easy life! My buddies and I spent all day throwing sharp sticks at a water buffalo. Never did hit the thing. Boy am I spent.

Men believe that everyone has a specific job to do, a job determined by God, nature, and, most importantly, men. It starts with physical differences. Men point to breasts as (a) a really good idea, and (b) proof that it is the woman's job to do every task associated with nursing children, which includes driving the car pool and balancing the checkbook.

As a Changed Man, I can assure you I have less of a Cro-Magnon attitude. Yet I do think that a lot of male–female relationships wind up being similar to life in the diorama, though probably with less back hair. This is because men model their relationships with women by observing how their mommies act toward them.

This is to be expected. Babies of both sexes regard their mothers as pretty darn significant, from both a social and mammalian aspect. I believe mothers treat sons differently from daughters, which makes the boys more difficult to remodel once they've been weaned.

Some women might suggest I say "if" they've been weaned.

Here's an example of that gender difference at play, in babies.

GIRL

NEW MOMMY:

What a wonderful girl baby! I'm going to take very special care of you. I will feed you and hold you. I will clothe you and keep the floor on which you crawl clean and free of small objects. When you are bored, I will entertain you. When you are sleepy I will put you to bed. I will bathe you and get up with you in the middle of the night when you are fussy. I love you!

NEW GIRL BABY:

(thinking) What a wonderful mommy! And when I get older, I will repay your kindness by helping you around the house. I will shop with you and pick flowers for you. I'll cuddle with you and hug you. I'll do my best to help you cook and wash clothes. I love you!

BOY

NEW MOMMY:

What a wonderful boy baby! I'm going to take very special care of you. I will feed you and hold you. I will clothe you and keep the floor on which you crawl clean and free of small objects. When you are bored, I will entertain you. When you are sleepy I will put you to bed. I will bathe you and get up

with you in the middle of the night when you are fussy. I
love you!

NEW BOY BABY:

(thinking) What a wonderful mommy! And when I get older,
I will expect the same treatment, so I'll get a wife. I love me!

I'll argue that men are also babies when it comes to, of all
things, babies. I know several men who have convinced their wives
they, the men, cannot clean up baby vomit because it "makes them
throw up." I can't decide which is more ridiculous: the excuse, or
the fact that some women let their men get away with it.

ESTABLISHING MY CREDENTIALS
AS AN EXPERT IN BABIES

It is probably shocking to most people to hear me declare that
men are babies. On what scientific basis, they protest, do I so slan-
der innocent infants with this comparison? Did I do one of those
blind tests, with a group of men in one room, a group of babies in
another, and then carefully observe them without even the doctors
being told which group was which?

Clearly not. I couldn't afford to put a bunch of males in a room
in my house, hogging my television and drinking all my beer, even
though I'm fairly certain I would have won a Nobel Prize for my research. But I do have some personal experience with both cate-
gories, having raised three babies and, prior to that, having lived in
the Sigma Chi house at college. (In my opinion, babies act more
responsibly and throw up less often than members of a fraternity.)

I was actively involved in the birth of all three of my children;
meaning, I stood around and watched them come out. I was rather
pleased with the process and went so far as to claim, as men often

do, that because I was in the vicinity of a successful project when it occurred, I was by and large responsible for how well things went.

My boasting came to the attention of my cousin Jen, who became pregnant after years of trying. Her husband travels extensively, but I'm pretty sure she limited her trying to when he was in town.

When Jen called to ask me if I would serve as the "backup birth partner" for when her husband was on one of his trips, I was caught in a quandary. It was an issue of conflicting priorities on two matters very dear to my heart. On the one hand, I was eminently qualified for the job. I loved my cousin Jen, and all it meant was going to a couple of Lamaze classes and then being available if she went into labor unexpectedly. On the other hand, her due date was in January and might conflict with the Super Bowl.

I decided that if it came down to it, I could probably catch the big game on a TV somewhere in the hospital, so I told her I would do it, which meant I soon found myself in a Lamaze class.

Jennifer is considerably younger than I, and we don't share any family resemblance—meaning she is rather attractive. A lot of people gave us coolly appraising looks as we sat down on the floor next to a mat.

"First," the instructor beamed, "please introduce yourselves, and tell us a little about how you met, how you came to be pregnant, et cetera."

This struck me as being sort of funny . . . Did we really want to hear how everyone came to be pregnant? So my snort of laughter drew the instructor's attention, and she singled me out. "Why don't we start with you, Mr. Funny Man," she suggested evenly, though she didn't really say the "Funny Man" part.

"Well, this is my cousin," I began.

Everyone in the room gasped.

"Her *husband*," I continued, glaring, "is some sort of traveling salesman."

"He negotiates oil leases internationally," Jen interjected.

I waved a hand. "Whatever." I cleared my throat. "When I was a young man . . ."

I was not even half finished with the story of my life when we had to take a break so that some of the pregnant women could use the bathroom. The instructor came over to me and asked if perhaps, in the interest of time, we could dispense with the rest of my biography and just stipulate that I was a very interesting person. I agreed, and when everyone had returned and settled down and the instructor announced that "Mr. Cameron is finished with his presentation," the class burst into applause. I was very gratified.

Lamaze is apparently the act of breathing so hard a baby pops out, so it's probably not a good idea to try it if you're not pregnant. Women practice breathing, while the men practice leaning over them and telling them to breathe. They have to have a special class for this?

At one point, I was told to squeeze Jen's leg to "simulate labor."

"I won't squeeze too hard," I assured her.

"That's okay. I need to get used to managing pain," she replied.

I shrugged. She had not had children, whereas I had, so I didn't blame her for being a little scared. "It's okay. It doesn't actually hurt all that much," I stated smugly.

"Really?"

"The whole thing is sort of overblown," I confided.

"I see." She looked thoughtful.

The instructor wandered over to make sure I was giving Jen's leg enough of a workout to simulate having a human being come out of her body. "Bruce says labor isn't really all that painful," Jen greeted her. Several men, their hands cramping from all the thigh clutching, glanced over hopefully.

"Is that so?" the instructor commented mildly. She was a stern-faced woman, tough-looking and muscular.

"I've had three children," I explained modestly.

We appraised each other. No doubt she wished she had let me finish with the story of my life so that I could have mentioned my reproductive experience and saved her from this faux pas. "So you had three children," she pronounced heavily. "You. You had them."

I got her point. "You probably think I look too young to have had three kids," I agreed.

"And you believe that labor doesn't hurt at all?"

I was glad to be asked the question. I paused, looking thoughtful so that I would appear, well, full of thought, and then answered, "I do believe it does cause some considerable discomfort, I suppose, but the problem is that women for the most part don't handle pain very well."

"Discomfort," the instructor repeated flatly. She gave Jen a pitying look, and then moved on to the next couple.

"You'd think they'd put someone in charge who knows something about it," I whispered to Jen. My cousin was very quiet, perhaps a little awed at how well I had conducted myself.

As luck would have it, I ran into that instructor less than a month later, but under far less pleasant circumstances.

It began in the morning. I was eating breakfast and staring out the window, trying to decide if I wanted to think up some procrastination strategies or wait until later to do that, when all of a sudden a twinge of pain flashed through my side.

"Ouch!" I cried. I fell to the floor, clutching my stomach. Mittens the kitten came over to sniff at me curiously. "Call nine-one-one," I gasped. I'd experienced this exact same type of pain before, and knew exactly what it meant: My body was getting ready to pass a kidney stone.

The cat, of course, couldn't be bothered to help me and went over to the corner to lick itself. So I called my dog, who came over to lick *me*. "No! Need . . . phone . . . ice . . . freshly laundered underwear for the ambulance . . . breath mints . . ." I panted. The dog heard the word "no," and slunk off guiltily.

I don't want to exaggerate, so I will simply say that the white-hot agony in my side was as if all the physical pain that has ever existed in the history of the world had combined to attack my abdomen. I crawled to the phone and called my younger daughter. "You have to take me to the hospital," I sobbed. "Code red. This is it."

"But it's my day off!"

I explained to her about all the pain in the history of the world, only I made it "the universe" instead so she'd know how serious this was.

With a sigh, she agreed to come over. Soon I was in her car, sweating and moaning and gasping, clutching the arm rests, and squeezing my eyes shut.

This is how I always react when she drives.

"I need to stop and pick up my dry cleaning," she told me.

"What? Are you crazy?" I stormed, speaking each word through a haze of what medical journals would categorize as "the pain of extreme torture." "I said this was code red. There are no other codes worse than code red. Aren't they teaching you anything in that college?"

"It's not my fault you chose to do this on a Saturday, so we're all going to have to compromise," she reasoned. "The cleaners close at noon today."

"What? *Chose* to do it?" I demanded. "Did the *Titanic* choose to hit an iceberg? Did the dinosaurs choose to go extinct?"

"What are you talking about?"

"Honey, I'm passing a kidney stone. It is like peeing lava with exploding teeth. Let's skip the cleaners, okay?"

"Oh, a kidney stone? You've had those before," she sniffed dismissively. "You lived."

By the time we pulled up in front of the emergency room doors, the pain was so bad I was certain other people could hear it. I was plunked in a chair while my daughter ran off to call one of her friends about some party.

"Well, who do we have here?" a voice asked softly from in front of me. I peered up out of my agony and saw, to my amazement, the Lamaze instructor.

"Kidney . . . stone," I grated. "Need . . . painkillers. Back rub." I toppled off the chair so she'd see I meant business.

"I'm the triage nurse in this unit. Do you know what 'triage' is, Mr. Cameron?"

I really find it annoying when people can't seem to get out of the instructor mode.

"Triage is the process of assigning priority to incoming patients," she lectured. "What you have is non-life-threatening. Several people ahead of you are dealing with more serious ailments."

I processed this. "I'll pay cash," I wheezed.

"We're very busy today. I'm doing the best I can to allocate resources where they are most needed."

"Is there some sort of nurse fund I could contribute to?" I suggested.

The instructor leaned over me. "I've had a kidney stone before, Mr. Cameron. Also two children. Labor hurt a lot worse. Understand what I am saying? Compared to pushing out a seven-pound baby, a half-gram stone is nothing. You can handle this." She patted me on the shoulder. "Practice your breathing."

I had it in mind to complain to the head of the hospital about this woman, but once I was back in the treatment room with an IV of morphine, I had no complaints about anything. I felt magnanimous toward everyone, languidly waving at them as I was wheeled down the hall. "Thanks, you're wonderful, I couldn't have done this without you," I told them.

The unfortunate thing about narcotics is that they eventually wear off, and I was sore for several days after this incident. With each twinge of after-stone echoing through my system, I recalled my day in the emergency room and the conversation I had with the woman I've come to think of as Nurse Satan. I imagined my poor cousin Jen believing that having me squeeze her thigh was somehow preparing her for the pain of giving birth. Squeeze her thighs! Probably I should have used a bench vise, or maybe just parked the car on top of her.

I am now completely remodeled when it comes to the topic of labor pains. Never again will I claim that labor doesn't hurt, because you never know when the person you talk to is going to turn out to be some psycho nurse with the power to deny you narcotics. From now on, I'm keeping quiet on the whole subject.

A SICKENING STORY

Not long ago I was felled by a virus that had all the symptoms of a serious illness: nausea, headaches, fatigue, and a strong addiction to daytime television. I crawled into bed with a box of tissues and the telephone, and began calling people. To my frustration, all I reached was voicemail.

"I'm really sick. I think I have a fever. I've got all this gunk coming out of me. It's really miserable. I threw up. Call me, I'd really like to hear what you think of these symptoms," I said.

Oddly, no one called me back.

Desperate, I phoned the office and asked to speak to Sarah. "I'm pretty sick," I concluded after I recounted all of the things going wrong with my body.

"It must be going around. I had the same thing two weeks ago."

"Oh, this is much worse," I assured her.

"Well. Sorry to hear it."

"So could you come over?" I pleaded.

"Why?"

"Well, you know. I'm really sick."

"You want me to come over and take care of you?"

"My mother used to feed me homemade chicken soup," I agreed.

She laughed. "You didn't exactly race over to take care of me when I was sick."

"I was busy!"

"Look, just drink plenty of liquids and get some rest, give your body time to recover," she advised.

"Is that what you did?"

"No, I went to work. Women don't get the luxury of lying around in bed when they're not feeling well."

"I'm not going to talk to you if you're going to be irrational."

She laughed again. "Well . . . maybe I can help. I just thought of something. It has a bit of a remodeling flavor to it as well."

"That's right, you took that massage class!"

"I'm not coming over; I've got to finish this article I'm working on. You just try to get some sleep."

"I thought we were friends," I complained grumpily. We said good-bye and I wandered despondently through the house, unable to believe life could be so cruel. When I was in the bathroom I noticed my eyes were all red and runny. This was a new symptom, so I sent out another volley of telephone calls.

I had drifted off to sleep when all of a sudden I heard my front door bang open and someone marching through my home. And then I was amazed to see my mother standing in my bedroom doorway. In a flash, I knew Sarah was behind this. She'd met my mother at our newspaper's annual "Instead of Giving Our Columnists a Raise We're Giving Them This Reception" reception, and the two of them talked for an hour about my mom's career as a sports journalist.

"Why didn't you tell me you were sick?" she clucked, coming into the bedroom. She held a hand to my forehead, which she has been doing my whole life, though she has never once commented on what it is she thinks she is feeling.

"Have you called your sister the doctor?" she asked.

I groaned. "No."

"Well, she's probably too busy with patients anyway. You know, she was telling me just the other day that even people your age are starting to go to medical school. Isn't that wonderful?"

"Mom . . . I'm a writer."

"Yes, but it is never too late." She looked around the room. "What on earth made you pick these colors?"

"Mom, what are you doing here?"

"I heard you were sick!" she explained brightly. "I realized there was no one here to take care of my little boy, so I rushed right over. I know you think you haven't got a friend in the world, but I'm the one person you can count on."

"Mom . . . I have friends."

"And don't thank me. This is just the job of a mother, to drop everything and take care of her children like I've been doing my whole life. I don't expect anything in return, not even on my birthday."

"Mom, I took you out to dinner on your birthday!"

"Did you see the flowers your sisters sent?"

"All of us sent, Mom, all of us," I corrected.

"Well, I know you can't be bothered with such things. You're too busy with your . . . activities." She gestured to the show muted on TV. "It's enough for me to be alone in the house with my memories, thinking of all the times I stayed up with you when you had colic."

"Why are you alone in the house? Where's Dad?"

"Have you given any more thought to Uncle Bob's offer?"

"Mom, I am not going to work in a shoe store."

"He offered to make you a manager, Bruce," she reproached. "Well, after a few years on the job, of course."

"I already have a job! I can't believe you'd want me to work for Uncle Bob instead."

"I just want you to be happy," she soothed.

"I am happy!"

"Of course you're not happy. Look at you, lying around in the middle of the day, watching soap operas. You're a grown man."

At this point I made a noise that was loud but incoherent.

"Well." She stood up. "I'm going to go downstairs and reorganize your kitchen. I don't see how you can prepare a decent meal in such a place. I hope that stack of bills on the counter doesn't mean you've fallen behind on your payments. You need to protect your credit, you know."

"Mom . . ."

"Your sisters have perfect credit!"

Within a few hours I was up, showered, and fleeing the house, claiming I had a meeting I'd suddenly remembered. My mother, beaming, told me she could come back later, but I assured her I was feeling fine.

REMODELING THE BIG BABY

When they enter into a committed relationship, most women are unaware that the man thinks it's sort of like an adoption: You're there to take care of him. It usually doesn't work the other way around, either. He'll watch you get out of bed with a fever to do some laundry or clean the kitchen, and his idea of trying to make things easier for you is to say, "Hey, why don't you leave that until later?" When he's sick, though, don't expect him to do anything but complain—he can't go to work, he's sick!

Follow the example in this chapter, though, and you'll remodel your man. Every time he catches a cold and needs babying, don't allow yourself to act like his mother—call in the original.

She'll know what to do.

9.

\- -- -

GADGETS, GIZMOS,
AND GEEGAWS

Men—Some Assembly Required

The world is a complicated place, with more modern devices being produced every day designed to decrease our manual labor and our garage space. Men are usually confused by the plethora of gizmos out there, and feel the only solution to their perplexity is simply to buy every single one of them. For example, you'll never hear a woman claim that she "needs" a plasma screen television. Yet the only men who feel they don't "need" such a thing are the 6 percent who already own one.*

A man believes he is the master of his machines, and to imply otherwise is to question his masculinity. This is why a man will spend four hours in the rain trying to open his locked car door

---

*This figure changes all the time as an ever larger group of people purchase plasma screen televisions—a group to which I really need to belong. So this percentage should not be considered accurate for very long, or even to begin with since I essentially made it up.

with a coat hanger instead of calling road service. The car is an extension of him, a member of his army who shouldn't be disobeying him. And naturally the bigger the army, the better. He'll buy something he doesn't need and then show it to his friends, who will conclude they need one, too.

I promise you that the first fax machine ever sold was purchased by a man. He bought it, brought it home, plugged it in, and then stared at it, waiting for something to happen. Eventually, he talked his neighbor Tom into buying one, too, so they could send messages like this:

FAX

From: **Bruce**
To: **Tom**

This fax has 1 page including this cover page. If you do not receive this FAX, please call me.

Message:

Hey Tom, this is a test.
Bruce

Next he called Tom and asked, "Did you get my message?"

At the very dawn of civilization, early humans learned to use clubs to beat on logs and transmit messages over long distances.* When someone got a new log, all the cave men would come over and admire it, especially if it had a bunch of cool features, like log

---

*There is no way to prove this is not true.

waiting and log forwarding. They'd stand around as the new owner proudly demonstrated his new toy.

"Great sound!" they'd shout over the thumping.

The new owner would pound out a log message to his next-door neighbor, then go over and ask, "Did you get my message?"

Men believe that their affection for gadgets automatically translates into an ability to install and operate them without reading the instructions. Women can't understand this because women believe that the purpose of a device is defined by its name, whereas men believe that the purpose of a device is to serve as an extension of the man himself. So a garage door opener, in a woman's viewpoint, should be quickly installed so as to open garage doors.

"But for a man," Sarah told me in the break room one afternoon as I stood pondering what I wanted from the candy machine, "it's as if a Zen-like relationship exists between himself and the new toy. He extends his hand, pushes the button, and the garage door rises. He's the God of garage doors."

"That's not it at all," I replied. I had found the candy bar I wanted and selected it, and now it was compelled to come to me, shoved forward to answer my summons. It fell to the retrieval bin with a satisfying thud.

"You should have seen Doug in the garage over the weekend. He played with the new opener for about an hour, the door going up, the door going down." Sarah raised and lowered her hand. "Why do men act like a simple project such as putting in a garage door opener somehow proves their manhood? He talked about it all during dinner. And, of course, it's not that we can park a car in there, his tools are still scattered all over the place. He probably expects me to pick them up. Why do men even need so many tools?"

"Well, you have to understand something about men, which is that your boyfriend Doug is an idiot," I explained.

Sarah stood up and put her coffee cup in the sink. "It's not that

I don't appreciate that he can fix things. But men always have this attitude, this sense they are smarter than women just because they know how to use a buzz saw."

"Oh come on, you don't know how to use a buzz saw?" I hooted.

"No, seriously, I don't. I don't even know what a buzz saw is," she said honestly. "What does it do?"

I frowned. "Well, it buzzes, for one thing."

"Ah."

"I don't think I could explain it so that you'd understand it," I informed her.

"Because you don't actually know?" she guessed.

"Well . . . yes, that's part of it," I admitted.

She clapped her hands. "Oh my God Bruce we *are* remodeling you!"

"I don't know what you're talking about."

"You admitted you don't know something about tools. To a woman!" she gushed.

I glanced around. "Keep your voice down, okay?"

She patted my shoulder as she passed out the door. "I've never been so proud."

"Oh stop."

Alone in the break room I sat down and thought about what Sarah had said. I realized she was right: Putting in a garage door opener did prove my manhood.

A MOST MANLY TIME WAS HAD BY ALL

I'll never forget when my friend Mike invited me over to share the experience of installing his garage door opener. This was a real step forward for us. We'd made other, minor recognitions of friendship—I'm godfather to his son—but this was the first time we'd shared something on this level.

The installation of the appliance was supposed to take an hour and a half, but it wound up taking us more than three hours. This was because there were two of us, we reasoned, and was no cause for alarm. Occasionally Mike's wife would come out to see how we were doing and would wonder out loud why it seemed like every time she did we were in the process of taking down something we had just put up. She obviously didn't understand basic engineering, so we would patiently explain to her that she needed to go get us more beer.

When we were done, Mike seemed a little concerned about all the leftover parts. He pointed to a notice on the box that read, "We did not include any extra screws, bolts, or pulleys. If you have some left over, you should have read the directions like your wife told you to." I assured Mike that this notice was not printed for men like us—some of the instructions were in French, for heaven's sake—and urged him to give his new gadget a try. He pushed the button, and we watched in awe as the metal track that was supposed to guide the mechanism to its destination instead folded in half, while the garage door shuddered and moaned and smoke poured from the electric motor. I was struck, at that moment, with a sudden insight: Mike and I had never even peeked at the directions, assuming that our native mechanical ability would enable us to put the thing together without error just by glancing at the photograph on the box. Clearly the device suffered from poor design, so the picture on the box was very misleading.

It is also possible that we didn't have the right tools. This is a very common reason why men are not able to complete projects successfully.

TOOLS AND WHY MEN NEED TO HAVE THEM

When Sarah asked, "Why do men need all of those tools?" she was not asking the right question. To a man, the question is, "What tools do you need?" and the answer is, "All of them."

Most men don't make enough money to buy all the tools they need all at once, which is why God invented revolving debt. Sometimes, though, men actually hit their credit limits, which is why God invented garage sales. At a garage sale, a man can pick up real bargains on used tools—tools that he might never have even realized existed. And yes, they cost money, but to a man this doesn't seem significant, because all he is doing is moving a tool from one man's garage to another. In other words, it seems less like a purchase than a transfer.

For a man just starting out, here's a very basic list of required tools.

THE TOOL	WHY A MAN NEEDS IT
Plumb Bob	A plumb bob is a heavy metal lump that dangles on a string. It is shaped like a teardrop but inverted so that the pointed part hangs straight down. Suspended from its cord, the plumb bob swings and eventually comes to a halt pointed at the center of the earth. Without a plumb bob, there is no scientific way to determine with absolute certainty in which direction the ground lies. You

(continued)

THE TOOL	WHY A MAN NEEDS IT
	can see how this could be a problem. Suppose, for example, a man is assembling a butcher-block table for your kitchen, attaching the legs in a most manly fashion. (I've done this myself, not to brag or anything, but it was a very masculine thing for me to do.) Without a plumb bob, the man might affix one or more of the legs in the opposite direction, so that he winds up with a tippy three-legged table and what appears to be a flag pole sticking up from one corner. (P.S. No one told me that butcher-block tables don't have a flag pole so I wish people would stop telling this story as if I'm some sort of idiot. I DID NOT HAVE A PLUMB BOB. That's the real lesson to be learned here.)
Level	A level is like a ruler with an eyeball in it. Tip the thing and the eye rolls up like a teenager being told she can't leave the house with her bra straps showing. Supposedly, if you center the eye in its little tube, anything lined up with the ruler's edge is flat. But "level" is an oxymoron, if you think about it. If the earth is round, can anything truly be level? Therefore, if the pictures a man just hung look a little crooked to you, you are clearly failing to take into account the curve of the planet, or maybe you are one of those flat-earth-society idiots.

(continued)

THE TOOL	WHY A MAN NEEDS IT
Hammer	A hammer is used to pound on things when a man gets frustrated. It's best to have stuff around that you don't mind him pounding on.
Circular Table Saw	This is a huge monster of a machine that makes all kinds of racket and couldn't be harder to move if it were bolted to the ground. It's used primarily as a way to establish which part of the garage belongs to the man, since wherever this thing sits, nothing else can go there.
Lathe	A lathe is a nifty device for creating artfully carved table legs, which people need to do almost daily, right? Buy a man a lathe and watch how happy it makes him, but be careful: If you ask him what sort of stuff he's actually making with the lathe, he'll get all moody.
Tool Belt	This is a wide leather belt from which all sorts of long, hard objects hang. If you can't figure out why this is so appealing to a male, you obviously don't understand very much about men.
Jigsaw	A jigsaw costs several hundred dollars (for the top of the line—and men always want the top-of-the-line jigsaw) and is used to create jigsaw puzzles, which can also be purchased for about three bucks at the local Wal-Mart.

Women who suspect that men regard tools as new toys are (a) insensitive toward male needs to be productive and creative, and (b) correct. Men certainly don't purchase a new tool for the toolbox with the intention of using it to fix broken things around the house, unless what's broken is the toolbox. One gadget in particular, however, is critical to a man's survival—without it, men would cease to exist.

CONTROL OF THE
REMOTE CONTROL

When I was growing up, our TV repairman was like a member of the family. He'd come over whenever the TV stopped working, or went "on the fritz" as kids of my generation called it. My father would get very irritated with me when I used this expression, as do my children. It is odd that the only hip generation extant is mine.*

Removing the rear cover and replacing some glowing tubes, the TV guy would fix the set, putting it off the fritz, I guess one would say, and enabling us to return to the wholesome family activity of watching murder shows.

Today a broken television is not an item for repair, but rather a problem of garbage disposal. When my current set went on the fritz, I was discouraged to discover no one was interested in coming to fix it. I mean, it wasn't like this was some old dog that needed to be put to sleep. This was my television, in front of which I'd spent many happy hours surfing reruns and sporting events. It was something of an old friend, and I realized I had grown so accustomed to seeing it in its spot, I couldn't bear to part with it.

---

*The French way of saying "on the fritz" is "sur la fritz."

Then I realized that as soon as I got rid of it I could get a new one, so I paid a guy twenty dollars to come and haul it away.

Now, something men can really do well is negotiate themselves through the ins and outs of a transaction, working every aspect of the deal. This haggling is often necessary—the salesman's job, after all, is to try to load you up with expensive options you don't need and charge you a premium price, whereas the wary consumer can usually save a lot of money if he is willing to stick to his guns.

I had my price range set—$200—and I wanted that to include tax. I knew I needed a remote control, of course, but wasn't really interested in picture-in-a-picture or any of the other stuff that sometimes comes with the more expensive models.

The TV salesman saw me eyeing the sets and came over. I told him I was interested in the unit I was looking at, which sold for $229. "A little pricey, though," I informed him sternly, putting him on notice that he was going to have to work hard to earn my business.

TV GUY:

Plus it has too small of a screen.

BRUCE:

True, but I'm not sure I can afford anything more.

TV GUY:

The sixty-inch is only $3,800.

BRUCE:

That's a lot more than I wanted to spend.

TV GUY:

It has picture-in-a-picture.

BRUCE:

I don't really need that.

TV GUY:

You really do.

BRUCE:

Oh, okay.

TV GUY:

This model here has protoplasmic myopathy and non-interlocated spasmastic propulsion.

BRUCE:

Well wait, does that cost more money?

TV GUY:

Sure.

BRUCE:

Oh, okay.

TV GUY:

You of course want the extra mesmerfication.

BRUCE:

How much is it?

TV GUY:

Only $800. But it is worth it.

BRUCE:

Okay.

TV GUY:

That's a total of $4,962, plus tax.

BRUCE:

Well hang on there, friend, just hang on. I want the tax included in the price, now, out the door. I'm paying a lot, so

I want you to step up to the plate a little yourself. I'm pretty firm on that. You need to do that or no deal.

TV GUY:

I really sympathize with you! But it's the government that charges the sales tax, not us.

BRUCE:

Okay.

TV GUY:

I'll throw in free delivery if you buy a DVD player.

BRUCE:

I already have a DVD player.

TV GUY:

But free delivery? And don't you want a *fresh* DVD player to go with your *new* TV?

BRUCE:

Okay.

TV GUY:

Great! Let's go pick out your home theater system!

Not long after installing the new machine, my daughters came over to watch it with me. My older daughter seemed disappointed that I had purchased something so large she couldn't borrow it, and my younger daughter was fixated on the cost of the thing.

"Why do you need something so expensive?" she demanded. "You could have bought me a car for that!"

"It's the only way I could get such mesmerfication," I explained. "What's that?"

"I'm not really sure."

They glanced at each other. I hate when they do that.

"Plus, it has closed-captioning. For the hearing impaired," I stated, appealing to her liberal sensibilities.

"What good is that to us?"

"It means we can have a conversation and I can still watch television," I informed her happily.

"Don't all televisions come with closed-captioning?" she asked suspiciously.

"On this television, the captions are really large," I countered.

"What?"

"Let's stop talking and just watch."

We settled in and seemed to be enjoying ourselves, when after a few minutes my daughters started squirming.

"Dad!" my older daughter hissed.

"What?"

"Would you please stop changing the channel?"

"What do you mean?" I replied, truly puzzled.

"You keep jumping channels! Let's just watch one thing!" she complained.

"Two things. You're forgetting picture-in-a-picture," I corrected smugly.

"Give me the remote," she ordered.

I gaped at her. "Are you crazy? A man does not surrender the remote control."

At that moment the phone rang with an important call, so I was out of the room for half an hour. When I returned, my daughters were watching some movie I knew I would hate because it had Hugh Grant in it. Yet oddly, when I held out my hand for the remote, they surrendered it without a peep, although they did exchange glances again.

I settled into my chair, extended my imperial hand, and expertly thumbed the channel button. In the blink of an eye, we were on another movie, a black-and-white one about two people who were eventually going to kiss. On to the next channel, which was a talk show about women's issues.

One of my daughters stifled a giggle. Frowning, I started flipping channels more rapidly. I got movie classics, women's channels, a Mexican soap opera, and a cooking show. My sports channels, of which I had signed up for a rather restrained forty-seven, never appeared, nor did the kung fu movie channel, or the monsters killing-and-eating people channel.

"Hey!" I shouted.

My daughters were laughing openly now.

"What did you do?" I demanded.

"Us?" they giggled.

Fuming, I went through all the channels again. Still stuck.

After my daughters left, I found the operating manual where they had put it and sat down with my head hanging, burdened by an irreconcilable conflict. On the one hand, I could sit around and watch women's shows all the time. On the other, I could read the manual. Neither of these actions seemed very manly.

I called my daughter and promised her I wouldn't use the remote while she's watching something if she'd come fix my television. Meanwhile, I've gotten sort of hooked on the Mexican soap opera. Apparently, two very stunning young women are forced to spend a lot of time in the hospital talking to each other at the foot of a bed. I can't tell what they are saying, of course, but I've inferred from their acting that it must be something like, "I can't change my facial expressions!" The camera then zooms in on a guy wearing a doctor's white coat who looks alternately grim and shocked. "You can't make a look like this?" he asks grimly. "Or this?" he demands, shocked. The women shake their heads. "No we can't, but we are very beautiful and come to the hospital every day dressed in provocative outfits," they respond expressionlessly.

If your man hogs the remote, you can emulate my daughters'

method and remodel him by reading the television manual, though I do think such a tactic takes unfair advantage of him.

LEAVE A MAN TO HIS OWN DEVICES

Though women might agree that men should have tools, there are other gizmos they feel are plainly ridiculous. For example, my father has a remote device that communicates with a sensor planted in the yard and advises him when the lawn needs watering. My mother doesn't think this has much real value, although it does save him from having to go through the effort of looking out the window.

When it comes to gadgets, women usually want to remodel their men for one of two reasons: (a) they don't want to waste any more money on new gadgets that do nothing to improve their lives, though clearly mesmerfication is worth the cost, and (b) men never pay attention to the manuals, which means they bring the things home and can't get them to work.

TIP〉 If your man is salivating over a new toy and seems determined to buy it even if he can't really say why he needs it, you can usually derail his scheme by cutting to the insecurity all men feel, which is that whatever they are buying, it isn't good enough.

YOUR MAN:

Honey, I need to buy an ultrasonic fish finder. It will enable me to locate fish, identify their species, calculate their weight and age, and determine the sort of food they're in the mood for. Plus it can locate enemy submarines, and is only $800!

YOU:

That's a great idea!

YOUR MAN:

It is?

YOU:

But are you sure you want to buy one now? What if they come out with one in a couple of months that locates schools of fish via satellite, and tells you which ones are hungry?

YOUR MAN:

Oh . . . well . . .

YOU:

I mean, you obviously need this, even though you don't have a boat, but wouldn't it make sense to ensure you are getting the very best one? You wouldn't like it if next week Tom came home one with of the satellite-enabled ones.

YOUR MAN:

You're right!

Getting your man to learn how to actually use the device he's just purchased is a bit trickier, as anyone with a VCR stuck on 12:00, 12:00, 12:00 can attest. There's a reason why the father of the modern computer is actually a mother, Admiral Grace Hopper. Her partner, Howard Aiken, might have wired the gizmo, but it was Admiral Hopper who invented the language so that people could actually use the darn thing. As far as the guys in the Pentagon were concerned, it was cool enough just to have this giant machine full of blinking lights—only Hopper thought maybe it might be more fun if it did something useful. Her invention of the first "compiler" eventually led to the creation of COBOL, the computer language that gave us the term "geek."

TIP ⟩ Here's how to remodel your man when it comes to his new toy. Say he's in the garage, attempting to install a new opener, and he doesn't have the instinctive feel for mechanical engineering that I do. Watching him, you know that he's doing something wrong. When you pick up the installation instructions and remove them from the sealed plastic pouch, you can quickly spot the problem, which is that he is putting it in upside down as my friend Mike did and for which I can't be blamed because the picture on the box was wrong. Now, how do you get your man to read the manual, which he obviously isn't going to do?

Try this: Approach him with the booklet open to the relevant page, and say, "Honey, can you explain this part to me? I just don't understand, because I'm a woman and you're a much smarter man who is putting the garage door opener in upside down."

He'll miss most of what you said because of his swearing at the way the stupid opener is manufactured, but he'll stop and look at you. "Huh?"

Show him the manual and repeat your question—without the ironic editorializing, please. He'll feel the need to explain it to you, so let him, and as he points to the picture in the book and then at the upside-down motor, he'll trail off, the thought occurring to him that there is something really wrong here.

This change won't be permanent; you'll have to repeat this process every time he comes home with some new labor-saving device.

But at least your garage door will open.

10.

— — —

THE KIDS WANT A COOL DAD

A Project That Was Doomed
from the Start

As a parent, I've witnessed firsthand the miraculous process by which my offspring went from being helpless little babies who looked to me for guidance in every single matter of importance in their lives to being adult-sized people who think it's their job to tell me how to live my life.

It doesn't seem to matter that my kids have already changed me. From the moment they came home from the hospital, they subjected me to sleep deprivation—a condition that certainly did not improve once my daughters started staying out late on dates. As teenagers, they introduced me to cash dispossession, followed by college-induced asset depletion and debt enhancement. Now, having at least legally passed out of their teens, my daughters like to entertain themselves with an on-going game of Maybe I Should Get My Masters, Life Was So Much Better When I Was in School

Being Supported by My Father. My son, in the meantime, is too young to have a driver's license, but he subscribes to magazines that feature automobiles that cost more than an island in the Caribbean. I've informed him that if I had the money to buy a Ferrari I certainly wouldn't give it to him, but he is undeterred. I fear insurance premiums, speeding tickets, and property damage will turn all of my income into outgo.

All this aside, my children in recent years have begun to agitate for me to become, in their words, more cool.

This is frankly offensive. I am totally cool. I am a cool dude guy, a hipster.

"Give me one example," I challenge my younger daughter, "of when I am not cool."

"Dad, you snap your fingers when you listen to music." She proclaims this the same way one would condemn a person who blows his nose on other people.

"That's because I'm grooving to the beat," I retort.

Her mouth opens in uncontrolled laughter. "Grooving?" she gasps.

I watch with cold eyes as she clutches her stomach and nearly collapses to the floor in a parody of mirth. It is all very exaggerated. "This is all very exaggerated," I inform her.

I find it ironic that the same individuals who used to sit in their highchairs in restaurants and throw peas at other diners now profess to be embarrassed to be seen in public with me because of the shape of my sunglasses. The same daughter who once screamed for an entire two-and-a-half-hour plane ride turns to me on elevators and hisses, "Dad, you're *humming*!" as if I'm bothering any of the other people, who are probably enjoying what is, after all, free entertainment. The same boy who threw a tantrum when I wouldn't let him go to preschool in his Spiderman pajamas now begs me not to wear my bicycle shorts in front of his friends.

When a cousin invites us all to her wedding, my children show up to foist upon me some unnecessary and unwelcome coaching on how I should comport myself.

"Okay, do not ask the DJ to play anything," my older daughter instructs, reading from a list they have prepared.

"Do not use the word 'jazzy,'" my other daughter adds.

"Don't try to shake hands as anything but an old white guy," my son admonishes.

"Oh, and don't drink," my younger daughter adds.

"Right," the other two affirm.

"Why not?"

They look at each other. "Dad, you get . . ." my older daughter starts gently, searching for the right word.

"Joyous," my younger daughter completes for her. They all nod.

"We hate it when you act like you're having a good time," my son explains.

"Why don't I just sit in the corner duct-taped to a chair?"

They seem to consider this, but ultimately reject it as impractical.

My younger daughter jumps up. "Okay, we came over here to teach you how to dance."

"What? Teach me? I'm an excellent dancer! Stop laughing!"

They put on a CD. "Okay. They'll play this song."

I frown. "That's not a song, that's someone talking while the same three notes play in the background."

"Oh, you mean you're not grooving to the beat?" my younger daughter wants to know.

"Okay, here's how you dance to this," my older daughter says. They begin moving in a fashion for which the word "gyrating" was invented. Through most of human history, women who moved like this were burned as witches.

"Good lord," I protest. "You mean I'll be pole dancing?"

"Oh stop. Now you try."

I gamely get to my feet. I close my eyes, feeling for the beat. The secret seems to be to raise one's hands above one's shoulders and then undulate along the length of one's body, thrusting the hips while turning the head from side to side. I'm pretty good at it.

"Oh my God you have to stop!" my older daughter shrieks. My son shuts off the CD player. They all look shaken.

"Okay, no dancing," they conclude. My older daughter puts it on the list.

"So you don't want me to dance or drink at this wedding. Anything else? Is it okay if I talk?" I inquire sarcastically.

They consider this. "Just don't tell any jokes," they advise.

THE HIPSTER DAD AT
HIS COUSIN'S WEDDING

The ceremony seems to be particularly successful—as a man, I gauge the beauty of the wedding by the number of women I see crying. I've also learned to gasp, "What a beautiful dress!" when I see the bride for the first time. All wedding dresses, no matter how hideous, are beautiful. This one seems to be about ten feet wide, as if it were bought strictly on the basis of how much storage space it offers.

At the reception I am seated with my daughters, which is a benefit of having older offspring. As teenagers, they can't stand to be seen with you. As they get older, they want to be near you so you'll look favorably on their requests for money. My son, though, has elected to sit at a table with a bunch of women from the bride's place of employment. She's a flight attendant.

He looks content.

"At my wedding, I want to arrive on a horse and carriage," my younger daughter muses dreamily.

Horse and Carriage Rental	$2,400

"Not me," my older daughter states. I look at her fondly. "I want to get married in June, on a lake."

Park Rental, with Lake	$3,600

"All the guests will float around in small rafts, while on the main boat, we'll stand and be married by a real ship's captain."

Small Navy	$8,900
Real Ship's Captain	$400, plus drinks for him and his crew
Dramamine for Dad	$2.95

"Then there will be a fireworks display. A big one, like they used to do in town for the Fourth of July before the liability insurance got too expensive."

Fireworks	$14,800

The waiter cruises past, and I snag a glass of champagne. My children scowl severely. "Just don't get all happy, Dad," they warn.

We enjoy a nice meal, salmon stuffed with shrimp stuffed with crab. The napkins are the same hues as the bridesmaids' dresses, a pale pink and white that seems to be the wedding's team colors. They pretty much match the salmon, though when I mention this my daughters shake their heads violently. Matchbooks with the bride and groom's names embossed on them are placed at every table, though the guests are admonished not to use them to smoke. Ice sculptures drip and flowers bloom. The father of the bride stands weakly at the bar.

When the music starts up, my children fix me with hard stares, glaring me into meek inaction. Then some huge disaster—apparently the white doves won't be arriving in time to fly in formation over the bride and groom as they get into the Mary-Kay-pink Due-senberg—summons all available women to the bathroom for crisis management. I find myself unsupervised, with no impediments to joy. My mood picks up considerably.

My daughters return to report that although the doves are still MIA, the albino llamas will still be trotting alongside the vehicle as it cruises past the trumpeters. I turn to my girls with a formal air, introducing them to the young men to whom I've been talking.

"This is Charlie. He owns his own business prevaricating salad moldings," I say, clapping my hand affectionately on the man to my right. He seems impressed that I remembered what he does for a living.

"Call me Andy," he says to my older daughter. "I'm in prefabricated side moldings."

My daughter replies that she works for a commercial printing company.

"You two have a lot in common!" I point out.

"Well . . . sure," Charlie admits.

"And this is Wholano," I continue, pushing a very handsome man toward my younger daughter.

"Wholirino," he corrects.

"Wolyreeno," I agree.

"Wholeeaho," he states.

"Wholiwayoo," I counter.

"Wholeeahoy," he claims.

"Wholiawaho," I enthuse.

My daughters shake hands with their new friends. I beam at them. "Boys your age!"

"Dad, can we talk to you for a minute?" my older daughter wants to know.

"And stab forks into your head?" my other daughter agrees pleasantly.

They drag me over by the DJ. "Dad, you're getting a little too happy, here," my older daughter says. "We talked about that, re-member?"

"And you are traumatizing us," my younger daughter chimes in.

"We just really don't want you introducing us to anybody to-night. Or ever."

"Charlie's a really nice guy," I say archly.

The music segues into a fast number, and my children grab my hands. "Do not snap your fingers! Do not groove to the beat!"

"I wasn't!"

"If you start dancing we will never forgive you." They look at each other, horrified. "And don't even think about asking the bride to dance! You wouldn't do that, would you?"

I refuse to dignify this with a response.

My daughters can't keep me pinned down forever. To my de-light, Charlie asks my older daughter to dance. I'm able to see her face as she is spun around because she's at least a foot taller than he is, and I laugh at how hard she pretends not to be having a good time. Another crisis—the bride is in tears because the rose petals that will pave the way to the Duesenberg don't match the bridesmaids' shoes—draws off my younger daughter, and my son is on the floor dancing with a stewardess. I sneak up to the DJ and ask him to play something from my era.

"Big band music? Tommy Dorsey?" he guesses.

"Of course not," I snap. "Disco? Bee Gees?"

He blanches, but reluctantly agrees he has something that might work. After a few more spins with Charlie, my older daughter breaks away and comes over to chat with me, a scowl on her face, just as a familiar rhythm fills the air. "Come on," I call gaily, "This is *my* music!"

I pull her out on the dance floor and go to work. She seems awed that I can move so fluidly. Several couples take one look at me and respectfully vacate the dance floor, undoubtedly feeling outmatched and also because I sort of run into them as I groove to the beat. My daughter calls something out in encouragement.

"What?" I pant.

"When we get home you are going to be so tortured!" she yells back. I don't know what this means, but assume it is some new, hip phrase.

"Yeah, I'm all tortured!" I agree euphorically. Her perplexed expression indicates she's astounded at how quickly I've picked up on the idiom.

The music ends, and I bow gracefully to those applauding, flattered they stopped serving long enough to watch.

I smugly note that later, when I ask the bride to take a turn on the dance floor with me, she seems delighted.

"You look so happy!" I tell her as we make our way out to center stage. This is another thing you're supposed to tell the bride, even if she's the fifth wife of Henry VIII and is aware of what happened to the other four.

She agrees, beaming. "The rice turned out perfectly!"

Later I find out that the rice grains the crowd will be tossing are each individually etched with the bride and groom's names, which everyone decides is a unique and lovely touch even if no one can actually see it.

As the music starts, I ignore the hand signals from my daughters, who appear to be communicating a desire to see me dismembered, and begin dancing energetically. It occurs to me that I can physically act out the lyrics of the song for the bride. When the singer croons "I close my eyes," I close my eyes. When he sings "My heart is heavy," I bend over, clutching my chest with the weight of it. When he sings, "I am drowning in a river, dark as a river of mud," I act that out too, so captivating the bride with my realistic portrayal of a man struggling to breathe in the black muck that she stops dancing and just stands there with her hand over her mouth.

It is, in all, a very pleasant evening, despite the fact that the llamas run away when the Duesenberg backfires. I drop my son at his mother's and deliver my daughters back to their places and never for a moment suspect they are plotting against me.

WHY DADS ARE NOT COOL (EXCEPT FOR ME)

I told Sarah about the criticism I'd gotten from my children because they couldn't see how cool I really was.

"Well, did you think your parents were cool when you were their age?" she wanted to know.

"My parents?" I laughed. "No! But I'm not like them."

"Of course not," she said levelly.

"They were from the fifties generation," I explained. "So they had the whole Eisenhower thing going on."

"Whereas you're more like Gerald Ford," she deadpanned.

"No! I'm more like, um, Shaft."

"Shaft!" she screamed. Some people in the break room glanced in our direction. "Oh my God." Tears were streaming from her eyes.

"I mean I'm that cool," I insisted, waiting for her to recover.

"I swear, Bruce, I just never know what you're going to say next," she told me, blowing her nose. "Shaft. Oh my."

"Really though, you don't think I need to be remodeled on this, do you? I mean, don't you think I'm cool?"

She nodded solemnly. "You're one *bad* mother," she agreed, doubling over again.

"No really, Sarah. Really. Come on, stop laughing. You don't think I'm like my parents, do you?" I pressed.

She regarded me with watery eyes. "No, I think you're cool."

"I mean really."

"No really. I really do, Bruce."

I examined her face suspiciously. "I don't know if I can believe you or not."

She shrugged. "I'm telling you the truth. That's how I feel, anyway. Your kids, I'm sure, have a different opinion."

MY CHILDREN'S REVENGE

For some reason I agree that I should spend a week with my children in Keystone, Colorado, learning to snowboard even though I am an extremely skilled skier from that lesson I took when I was in college.

"Dad, my girlfriend learned how to do it in like less than an hour," my son chides.

"You're not going to goad me into something just because a girl can do it. I am far too secure in my masculinity to feel threatened by such obvious manipulation," I inform him in my best Changed Man mode.

"Don't feel bad just because she's more athletic than you are," my son commiserates.

We arrange to spend a week in a condo near the slopes via some deal made by my newspaper editor, who wants me to write a column about the whole thing. "If you break a leg, that would be even funnier," he tells me.

"If I broke bones, I probably wouldn't be able to write my column for a month, and then where would you be?" I point out. His look indicates he doesn't think it would actually be that big of a problem for the paper.

My children dismiss the idea that I should take lessons from a professional instructor who has been specifically trained to deal with people like me who are physical risk-takers who don't want to get hurt.

"It will be really fun to teach you, Dad!" my younger daughter proclaims with so much joy I am instantly apprehensive.

First stop is the rental place to outfit me with the equipment I'll need. "So dude, what kind of board do you want?" the snowboard technician wants to know.

"Do they come with airbags?" I ask hopefully.

"Dude!" he responds.

I absorb this.

My son steps forward to help, explaining that I am like a beginner dude who needs a shorter board because, like, dude, and also a helmet because obviously, dude. I'm given a pair of ridiculously huge boots so that I walk like a Herman Munster dude, and we head to the slope.

In this case, "slope" means nearly flat surface. An area half the size of a football field is littered with beginners who are standing stock still, unable to build enough momentum even to fall down properly. "Oh, I think I'm a little more advanced than this," I observe smugly.

"Why don't we try it here once, and then if you want, we can go to the expert slopes," my older daughter suggests. I glance at her suspiciously, but her return gaze is open and innocent.

To get up the hill, the beginners step onto a conveyer belt that slowly chugs to the top, a moving sidewalk that I am able to mount after about nine tries. My children are behind me. "When you get to the top, sort of lean forward," they shout.

"Okay!" I call back to them.

"Don't try to turn!"

"Okay!"

"Go straight!"

"Look, would you just let me do this?" I snap. We're nearing the top. I lean forward. The sidewalk ends, and I'm pushed gently onto the surface of the snow. I fall as if shot.

"Are you okay, Dad?" my children ask anxiously.

"Why is everybody grinning?" I demand churlishly.

By clutching at my daughters and sort of using them like crutches, I manage to haul myself to my feet.

"Ready? Okay, let go. You can let go now, Dad. It's okay to let go. Let go," they tell me.

From this vantage point the bunny hill is a terrifying spectacle, a ferocious vertical drop. "You guys ready to go somewhere for lunch?" I ask weakly.

As it turns out, a snowboard operates on much the same principle as surfing, only in this case someone has taken the surfboard and is beating you with it.

"Just do *this,* Dad," my children advise, demonstrating a simple move that I am able to determine is completely impossible. There is plainly something defective with my equipment. The length of the board serves as a lever, flipping me onto the snow with a collision similar to what would happen if I was just standing there and decided for no reason whatsoever to fall flat against the ground from atop a school bus. Due to the compacting effect of the hundreds of middle-aged men who have crashed on it before me, the snow has the same cushioning properties as the floor of an airplane hangar. Lying there, I realize that for the first time in my life, I can actually feel my liver and my spleen, and they both hurt.

I am five feet nine inches tall. The slope is a hundred and fifty feet long. I must therefore fall twenty-six times before I'm at the bottom and can do it again. Each time I succumb to gravity, I develop another of what scientists refer to as an "impact crater." Before long the only part of me that isn't in pain is my helmet.

"I don't think you're doing it right," my older daughter states helpfully.

"No, really?"

The only time I am able to remain upright on the board for more than just a few seconds, I begin taking on speed. For the first time that day, I begin passing people, who stare at me in fear. "Hey, I'm doing it!" I shout.

"Dad, turn! You have to turn!"

I consider this. Thus far that day, "to turn" has been synonymous with "to fall." This is not appealing. However, I'm rapidly moving to the right edge of the slope, where a large tent has been erected for some sort of on-site promotion. Reluctantly, I decide it is preferable to avoid crashing into the picnic, and prepare to execute a turn. I lean back, just as instructed.

Nothing happens.

"Dad!" my son wails.

In front of me is a huge inflatable beer can, ten feet tall and held in place by guy wires. I wonder if anyone else sees any irony in the fact that I might die by colliding with a giant beer can.

"Hey!" one of the picnic-goers calls at me. He waves his arms.

"Oh, I do see you," I assure him.

He throws himself out of the way and I hit the beer can with full force. It is the softest thing I've crashed into all day. I embrace it as if it is a sign from heaven.

My daughters cruise up behind me, apologizing to people on my behalf for scaring them and hugging their beer can. I untangle from the wires and they escort me back to the moving sidewalk, lecturing me on what I did wrong.

By the time my son suggests we go inside for lunch, I've learned enough from my mistakes to know I don't want to come back out. My hands tremble as I pull my wallet out of my jacket pocket to pay for a twelve-ounce version of the can of beer that saved my life. I'm grateful there's a bar, though I'm disappointed they don't sell Vicodin.

I'm barely able to eat dinner that night. Just raising my fork to my lips takes an effort that simply doesn't seem worth it. The kids pile out the door to take in a movie while I ease myself into bed. I'm moaning as quietly as I can, but someone pounds on the wall from the room next to ours, anyway.

The body is a miraculous construction. During the night, my internal organs go to work on the various injuries I've accumulated during a day of abuse, replacing all of the sore spots with an immobilizing stiffness. The next morning I've developed something I never expected to experience at my age: rigor mortis.

"Dad, you're going to be late!" my daughter calls to me.

"No," I tell her, "I'm going to be absent. I can't move."

"Do you need me to come help?" she asks, concerned.

"No, I don't want to move," I tell her. "You go ahead. I'll lie here alone and in pain, not being a martyr, while you guys enjoy your week. I'll just stare at the ceiling, waiting for you to get back so my life can have some sort of meaning."

"Okay!" she agrees gaily.

Once they are out of there, I contemplate my fate. With a little bit of grunting, I'm able to reach the remote control, and the TV comes on to show me a film on snowboarding from helicopters. Watching people drop straight down the powdery slopes, my eyes widen in shock. Now I know why I am in such pain: I didn't have a helicopter!

THE LESSON IN ALL OF THIS

My children want a cool dad, which is to say, cool in some other way than I already am. They are learning that you cannot remodel your own father except by accident. Back your car into the shrubs, and for the next forty years he'll remind you to be careful while driving in reverse; lose an expensive tool of his and he'll forever be reluctant to let you borrow another one. You've changed him, all right, but probably not the way you'd like.

My older daughter postulates that when men get to be my age they lose so much cool that "just by being there they can suck the coolness right out of the room." Yet this ridiculous theory hasn't prevented her and her siblings from providing me with all sorts of advice on how I should behave in public. Usually, as with what turned out to be the completely toxic sport of snowboarding, the results are just not worth the pain.

My children have changed me in a lot of ways, but not in any they find particularly desirable. No matter how much effort they put into it, they cannot seem to make me more cool.

They can only punish me for trying.

II.

\- \- \-

DATING AND ROMANCE

And Other Things
Men Can't Really Do

Dating is the process during which two people share stress, awkwardness, and disappointment in order to determine the degree by which they each need to lower their standards. It differs markedly from courtship, the process in which a man behaves in a way that is highly ritualistic and very temporary in order to woo a woman, and from romance, which is a brain state peculiar to individuals who are falling in love, already are in love, or who have consumed a certain type of mushroom. Dating is more like accumulating points that can then be traded for exciting prizes. When women say they hate dating, it is because they long for courtship. When men say they hate dating, it is because they'd prefer to dispense with the whole process and go straight to the awards ceremony.

This isn't to say men don't want love. But men believe that true love happens more or less by accident, without calculation and hopefully after at least one incidence of sexual intercourse. They certainly don't see how courtship helps anything.

They're like my dog. Hold a doggy treat in your hand and the stupid animal goes crazy, running through his entire repertoire of tricks—sitting, barking, holding up his paws in supplication, and slobbering on your pants—without being asked. He doesn't comprehend why any of this behavior matters. He just wants the treat, and is trying whatever his dim brain can think of so that you'll give it to him.

Next time a man brings you flowers or candy, it's a pretty good sign that he would hold up his paws and bark if you asked him to.

IT STARTS OFF HOPELESS AND GETS RAPIDLY WORSE

I've read that men are from Mars—that is, they come from a lifeless planet where the surface temperature ranges from 30 degrees to –200 degrees—and women originally hail from Venus, which is a steamy, oxygen-less planet where the barometric pressure would crush an aluminum can. No wonder men and women can't get along with each other: They're both dead.

My belief is that until someone comes up with a third gender, men and women are often going to wind up with each other. Whether you're dating, seriously involved with, or are married to a man, remodeling him so that you can capture a little romance is mostly a matter of educating him about what you want.

As a Changed Man, I have pondered this situation and have reached the conclusion that the reason men don't know what women want is because the biggest thing women want is for men to already know what women want.

In other words, women don't want to hold out a treat and have a man slobber on their pants. They want him to figure out how to infuse their date, their relationship, their marriage with more romance. And by "figure out" I mean to take the radical step of actually paying more attention to her.

Take, for example, gifts. There is only one type of man who is good at buying gifts: men with secretaries. The rest of us depend on full-page ads declaring "Don't Forget Valentine's Day" to remind us when it is time to get a woman a present. The ads usually depict suggested items for purchase, which worked well for us until building supply companies got into the act. "Get Her a Circular Saw!" the advertisements urge. Now this we feel qualified to buy! Hey, it must be okay, we read it in the paper.

If men are bad at gifts, they are usually worse at cards. Men just don't understand the purpose of cards. When they are attached to a present, they just slow down the process leading to the payout. When they are sent by themselves, they seem to be screaming, "No matter what it says on this card, I didn't love you enough to buy you a gift!"

As a Changed Man, I have learned that there are three sentiments a man can express that will do more to win a woman's heart than all the cards produced by Hallmark. They are:

1. You're right. I'm wrong. I'm sorry.
2. Tell me what you think.
3. Well, enough about myself . . .

If the purpose of cards is to express what men think, what's missing from the shelves is something like this:

I may have acted stupid
I may have acted crass
I probably was insensitive
Or been a horse's ass.

I look at other women
Swill beer or booze or worse
Got tons of lousy habits
I scratch and fart and curse.

Let you do the housework
'Cause I just don't care
And when I put on underpants
My threads are really bare.

My socks just missed the hamper
My stories are a bore
And when it's time for intercourse
My play is lacking fore.

I cannot find the mayo
Upon the fridge's shelf
And hardly do I talk with you
Except about myself.

I may have played Nintendo
For fourteen hundred hours
And shied from all commitments
Forgot to buy you flowers.

In all these faults, I have to say
I did the best I can
And probably won't improve at all
You see, I am a MAN.

This goes to the heart of the main problem with attempting to remodel a man: Men believe they are the way they are, that it is their nature, that it can't be changed, that it is even sort of cute. It's as if your kitchen refused to allow you to replace the linoleum.

You probably think you've been very direct with your man, but he probably finds you so subtle as to be totally obscure. To remodel him, you must have a program.

A CHANGED MAN'S PROGRAM TO BEING SPONTANEOUS WHEN IT COMES TO GIFTS AND CARDS

"So, are you enough of a Changed Man to take on a real challenge?" Sarah greeted me one day. I'd been working on a column and was just on my way into my editor's office, holding a sheet of paper on which I'd written the memo explaining why my column would be late.

"So, you admit I'm a Changed Man, eh?"

"No, but I admit you're at least trying. My boyfriend won't even make the effort."

"That's because your boyfriend is a tree trunk," I explained kindly.

Sarah told me that Doug had actually called her from the store and asked her if she would like him to buy her a card for her birthday, or if a gift was good enough! Pleased that she was asking me for advice, I decided to, well, show off, and create a system for her boyfriend to help him be spontaneous.

"So he can read?" I said skeptically. When Sarah gave me a look, I grinned and told her I would get right on it, giving me another reason to avoid working on my column—my friend had an emergency!

"Dear Doug," I wrote, "I am sorry to hear you are such an idiot."

Okay, that was a little too blunt. Doug might be a jerk but he was a *huge* jerk, and I didn't want someone like that mad at me. I tried again.

Dear Doug,

Women are mysterious creatures to men like us, full of "needs" and other foreign impulses. This is one of the reasons why you probably feel, as do the rest of us, that you don't deserve a woman like Sarah as a girlfriend.

Was that going too far? I pictured Doug standing slack-jawed in his garage, watching the door go up and down for an hour, and decided I was okay.

Sarah, as you know, is clever and fun. No one has ever used these words to describe you, though I suppose you've been told more than once that you are "large."

There. He probably was just starting to get a little riled when I calmed him down—no man has ever objected to being called large.

What Sarah wants from you is spontaneity, which is hard for you because it requires . . .

A brain? A personality? The ability to process those "thoughts" that everyone else keeps talking about?

. . . you to think like a woman.

Perfect!

Since this is impossible for a man like you, I'm offering you a secret, Changed Man System so that you'll be capable of spontaneously sending gifts and cards. Read through this, moving your lips as much as necessary, and let me know if you have any questions.

A Secret System to Help Doug
to Be Spontaneous

First, go to the store and purchase twelve greeting cards. Try to find a section of the display that has soft pictures and words in cursive. Avoid "gross humor" or Pamela Anderson because (a) women do not appreciate receiving this sort of card, and (b) you'll wind up spending your whole day messing around reading butt jokes and looking at photos of Pammy in a bathing suit.

It doesn't really matter what the twelve cards say, though I should warn you that some of them are completely blank inside, which is totally worthless. Sending Sarah a blank card is worse than no card at all, because then she'll think you are telling her something very significant even though what you said was nothing. Try to find cards that show people walking on the beach at sunset; this is apparently very big with women. (If you don't believe me, read the personal ads sometime. The women all want a man to walk on the beach with them at sunset, even the ones who live in Kansas.)

Next, get a calendar and a dart. You're going to like this part. Open the calendar to January, and throw the dart at it. Take a card and write on its envelope the date you speared with the dart. Flip to February and do the same thing, and then on to the next month. Do *not* start to track your score by adding up the dates, because then you'll start shooting for the end of the month and the whole point here is to be random. Do *not* challenge some other guy to see if he can do any better. It is okay to make crowd noises with every throw, and if after you've done December, you want to declare yourself Champion of the World, fine, I won't tell anybody any different.

Now shuffle the cards and pull out six at random. Write the letter "G" on the backs of these six.

Finally, pack up all twelve of the cards and give them to someone you trust, like your mother. Ask her to give you the cards back on the dates specified.

When you receive a card, check to see if it has a "G" on it. If it does, go buy a gift. Then mail the card and the gift to Sarah.

In this way, you'll be totally surprising and spontaneous and thoughtful!

MEETING MEMBERS OF A SEX DIFFERENT FROM YOUR OWN

Men spend a lot of time discussing what will attract women, often focusing on the pickup line. To a woman, an attempt at a pickup feels like a man has thrown his net in the water and is looking to drag in any female unfortunate enough to get herself caught. To a man, a pickup line is more like a lure cast out into the river. If a female is attracted to it, perhaps she'll bite. Once hooked, he'll persuade her little by little to come to the side of the boat, reeling her in.

Both of these perspectives are offensive to women.

If you're the type of person who understands women—in other words, a woman—you might wonder why men think they need some sort of practiced line to help introduce themselves to a female-type person in the first place. If men were honest and sincere from the beginning, wouldn't they do a lot better? Here's a typical opening line, overheard in a bar. A man has walked across the room and slid up next to a woman with whom he'd exchanged glances.

MAN:

Hi, um, I noticed you were drinking the little . . . the beer, the microbrew that they make here. I think it's wheat?

WOMAN:

It's a wheat ale, yes.

MAN:

Is it any good? I mean, you like it?

Woman Seeking Man

Single Female Wanting to Find Life Partner. If you are tired of searching for that special someone and want to meet your soul mate, let's open our hearts to each other and discover if we were meant to be. The man I desire is gentle and kind, is happy in his life and wants someone to share it with. I crave long nights where the light comes from a candle and the heat comes from our love.

Put a message in a bottle and e-mail me about your hopes and dreams. If you're that special person, we'll know it. Photograph available to serious inquiries only.

WOMAN:
It's all right.

MAN:
Well, you're almost finished, do you . . . Can I buy you another one, maybe?

WOMAN:
Okay.

MAN:
I'll have one, too.

Well, it's hardly Shakespeare, but it worked because the woman was fairly receptive and because the conversation was about something that all men have an emotional reaction to: beer. Would it really have been better if the man had been totally honest?

MAN:
Hi, I was across the room looking at your ass and I wondered if we could have sex.

WOMAN:
Okay.

Ask a hundred men if this sort of honesty is a good idea, and they'll all respond yes, if this is what is meant by an honest relationship, they want very much to experience it. In fact, they want honest relationships with most of the women they meet.

Of course, a bar is not usually the best place for a woman to find her ideal mate, unless, perhaps, she's hoping to land an alcoholic. But men think bars are perfect, because the longer they stay there, the wittier they feel. So men go to bars and become so irresistibly hilarious they believe there's not a woman in the place who

Man Seeking Woman

Let's Party! If you are looking for someone who knows how to have fun you have come to the right place! Want to break a few rules? Come on, no one's watching, and even if they are . . . who cares?

I have a 750 cc Honda V Twin SOHC (see picture). Want to take a ride? The second picture is of me and my friend Bobby. I don't know who the girl in the middle is (ha ha).

If you think you're ready for a man with a "let's do it" attitude, send me a picture of yourself in a bathing suit or something, and I'll write back.

wouldn't want to go home with them, even if it turns out there's not a woman in the place. Thus they manage somehow to obtain positive reinforcement for a behavior that generates nothing but negative results. Is there any wonder that men are bad at romance?

The advent of the Internet has taken the awkward act of encountering eligible mates in social situations and put it where it belongs: at home. But reading the personal ads posted to matchmaking Web sites suggests that each gender brings into this new medium a different set of expectations.

As far as advertisements go, I'd say both of these reveal a certain lack of market research. Given the difficulty men and women seem to have in getting together, it's pretty amazing that the planet has an overpopulation problem.

Yet dating does happen . . . even to me. But I wouldn't have to be a Changed Man to tell you it rarely has seemed worth the effort. From the very beginning, the whole experience has been nothing but painful.

MY FIRST DATE

The very first time I asked a girl for a date, I didn't even realize that was what I was doing. In fourth grade I'd fallen in love with a strawberry blonde named Susie, and I was still totally smitten by seventh grade. By then the rules of engagement had changed: All through elementary school I'd been able to flirt by pulling on Susie's pigtails and to declare my love by hotly claiming to my friends that I hated all girls in general and Susie in particular, but by junior high boys were exchanging notes and glances and were even holding hands with girls. I was doing fairly well in the passing of notes; even then I was interested in the written word. Here's an example:

> Dear Susie:
>
> Hi! I am writing this in math class! I am bored with math! Do you like math? I don't like math very much. It is so boring! Boring, boring. I don't see how it applies to real life.
>
> Where are you going to sit at lunch? I'd ~~love to~~ ~~like to~~ be okay with sitting with you!
>
> I have to go! Bye!
>
> Bruce

But I was pole-axed with embarrassment over the idea of holding hands or kissing or anything physically intimate. Not yet afflicted with testosterone poisoning, I didn't want to do anything with or to Susie, other than to see her and talk to her every single day.

Susie, on the other hand, was quickly leaving elementary school behind. Her shirts were changing their configuration, becoming less aerodynamic in front, and more capable of inducing turbulence. Her hips were becoming curvy; she no longer looked as if she could wear my blue jeans. Other boys were starting to notice her, and she seemed very cool to the idea that I was still hanging around trying to tug on her pigtails.

I had to do something. Contemplating even a single day without Susie was worse than math class—it didn't seem like real life at all. I was starting to feel a crushing sensation in my chest, a shortness of breath, a dizzying lack of blood in my brain whenever I caught a glimpse of her talking to another boy.

One of the local churches regularly sponsored an event called Teen Town. It was considered a very grown-up place to hang out because everyone went there and danced to live, and frankly awful, music by a high school band. Grade schoolers were not allowed.

Asking a girl to Teen Town meant only that you would meet her there. But it was scheduled, arranged: You would wait for your girl by the coatrack and when she arrived, she would walk straight over to you instead of plunging into the impenetrable circle of chattering girls that usually formed at parties. You would hang up her coat and buy her a soda. It was very ritualized and awkward. I'd watched other boys go through it and thought it looked repugnant.

It was, I now realize, courtship.

Despite my dread of the whole experience, I resolved to ask Susie to Teen Town before some other boy beat me to it.

Etched into my mind as clearly as any other psycho-trauma I've ever suffered is the gut-wrenching moment I saw Susie sitting alone at a library table and realized that my time had come. All I had to do was walk across the room and ask her to meet me at Teen Town that Saturday.

Here's a blow-by-blow description of how my brain directed the action:

Okay, she's right across the room. Hold up, don't move yet. Just stand and stare. Okay, give a little stutter step, now stop. Hold. Hold. Okay, she's raising her eyes! Look away, look away! Okay, stare intently at the blank wall. Keep staring, act very interested. Now, slow sideways glance. Oh my God she's looking right at us! Look away! No, wait! Look back. Mouth, give us a shaky, sickly smile. Let's have a little tremor in the lips. Good. I want a half wave, sort of lame. Legs, start walking. Sweat glands, heat 'em up, let's do armpits and forehead. Okay, we're at the table. Full blush, starting now. Clear throat. Let's drum a little on the tabletop.

SUSIE:

Hi!

Okay, let's open the mouth, but don't say anything. Hold it . . . hold it . . . Okay, let's do a "hi," end it in a squeak.

BRUCE:

Hi. (squeak)

Good! Now, foolish grin. Let the awkwardness build. Excellent. We feel like a complete and utter moron. Let's make it even worse—cue voice.

BRUCE:

Hi.

SUSIE:

Hi.

Perfect! We now not only look stupid, we sound stupid! Good work. Now, I want a blurt, awkward as we can make it, followed by a harsh intake of breath, so that we sound mentally ill. Ready?

BRUCE:

Susie? I wonder if this weekend . . . (gasp).

Name the day, but stutter it a little!

BRUCE:

Sss-Saturday, if you wanted to go to Teen Town. I mean, with me.

Now, let's do a real clumsy clarification before she can say anything!

BRUCE:

I mean, you know, meet me there. Not with me, but, you know.

Excellent, I've never heard anything so lame. Okay, she's thinking about it. She's going to say yes! Panic! Panic!

SUSIE:

Okay.

Let's get the heck out of here now! Retreat! Retreat! Wait, wait, stop, we have to say something. Let's sound really formal and dorky.

BRUCE:

Very well.

Inspired! Where did that come from? Has any kid our age ever said the words "very well" in the history of the world? Have we got tape on that? Okay, let's start playing the tape as we turn and stumble away. Walk into the chair behind you, good! Oh great, she's laughing at us. Keep hearing yourself saying "very well." Good job, everyone.

The next Saturday, I showed up early so that I would have plenty of time to sweat completely through my shirt. The band was just getting started, sounding as if they'd never actually seen musical instruments before. A couple of boys were playing Ping-Pong.

I never understood them, the boys who came to all the parties and to Teen Town and then spent their evenings working the Ping-Pong table as if getting ready to play the Chinese team in the Olympics. They would not even look up, so intent were they on the game in front of them—an errant glance and they might notice there were girls in the place, which I suppose would wreck everything.

Susie's arrival caused within me a complete change in body chemistry. I was unprepared for her to be wearing makeup, for her to be so devastatingly pretty and grown-up. I was wearing the same clothes I wore everywhere else, and felt scruffy and insignificant as I watched her come down the stairs into the church basement. We were entirely silent as I threaded a hanger through her coat and hung it on the rack, like two spies on a deadly mission. I took her to the refreshment stand, finally speaking to her to ask her what she wanted. I then stiffly completed the transaction for a Seven-Up, handed it to her, and watched her drink it like I was a nurse making sure a patient finishes his medicine.

And then, for a while, things got miraculously, gloriously better, so wonderful I didn't spot the disaster building until I was in the middle of it. We went out and danced, I guess you'd call it. Susie didn't complain, though, as I spastically jerked my limbs to what sounded suspiciously like the same three songs played over and over. I even danced during the drum solo.

I was totally unprepared for the slow dance, but Susie seemed to have been expecting it, and stepped forward and put her arms around me as if it were not the most audacious thing in the world. I didn't know any slow dance steps, so it was more of a swaying clinch, but it was the first time in my life I'd held a girl that close, and I was swept away.

Less innocent times lay in my direct path, but at that moment I was nothing but a boy experiencing the sweet taste of first love. The only way I can think to describe it is that it felt as if my blood had turned into melody, and was coursing through my veins as light as musical notes lifting into the night air.

The band ran out of energy and shamefully put away its instruments. The lights came up, but no one left. I was uncertain what to do next, but Susie led me over to the metal chairs scattered to the side of the room, where people were gathering in small, whispering knots. After all the screeching from the amateur guitars, the silence seemed overly loud, though gradually I realized that a steady clacking sound was emerging from the Ping-Pong room.

We sat in an area that seemed—by common but unspoken agreement—to be the couples' section of the room. No one was saying much. A few kids were nuzzling, and then . . .

And then I realized with a shock that people were kissing. A giant make-out session was gathering force and I was at the center of it. Susie regarded me with puzzled expectation.

This would be my first kiss. I was sitting on a metal folding chair in a church basement, the lights so bright we could have used the place for brain surgery. I felt everyone was staring at me, waiting to see if I kissed as badly as I danced.

I couldn't do it. Several minutes passed, pleasant as rope burn, before Susie's eyes widened in understanding. I watched helplessly as the jury in her mind took less than a minute to find me guilty of gross inadequacy, and the sentence was read back to me by a subtle hardening of her posture, a clear withdrawal of her affections. Less than twenty minutes ago I'd been clutching her to me in a swoon of adoration, and now, just like that, she was gone from me, all because I wouldn't press my lips against hers in the acid, noonlike glare of Teen Town.

I was so swiftly excommunicated from her life it felt like what is commonly referred to as "explosive decompression." My notes bounced back to me unread, and Susie would veer into the girl's bathroom the moment she saw me approaching from down the hallway. I boldly tried phoning her at home—another first for me—but she would not accept my calls. The third time I tried, her father expressed his opinion that I should choose between leaving her alone or dealing directly with him, and I got the message.

The next Saturday I was as compelled to go to Teen Town as a salmon is to swim upstream, my lips ready to do whatever it took.

Alas, Susie was there with an eighth grader who clearly felt no embarrassment about a little smooching under the klieg lights.

Their dancing was less about hugging and more about groping, and to my extreme distress, Susie seemed okay with it all. More than okay, in fact.

I retreated to the entrance to the Ping-Pong room and darkly watched my love and her new beau all night. The boy was oblivious to my presence, and Susie's one glance in my direction was so full of merciless apathy I almost sank to my knees.

Nobody asked me to play Ping-Pong. They could tell from my expression that I would have turned it into a contact sport.

Though I wasn't aware of it at the time, this was one of my very first experiences in becoming a Changed Man. I realized that what Susie desired was natural, even normal. Susie just wanted to be touched, kissed, and grabbed, and had I but a little courage, I would have kept her love.

As is so often true in life, the lessons I learned from my encounter with Susie were not applicable to any other girl I dated for the next several years, most of whom avoided my lips and pushed my hands away. Then I became an adult and suddenly all the fumbling and kissing was called foreplay and I was supposed to be good at it even though I'd never been able to do it with anyone. People my age don't make out without a clear goal in mind, it seems, so relationships with women have something of an all or nothing feel to them. Which is a bit sad: Sometimes what I really want to do is experiment a little with the sort of thing that Susie wanted from me in Teen Town. No purpose, no goals, no significance, just a little making out, only on more comfortable chairs.

STILL STUNNED

There's a footnote to the story about Susie. When I was a junior in college I came home for a visit. I hadn't seen Susie for nearly a whole decade, but I spotted her in the Christmas crush at a local mall. I stopped dead, my brain flooding me with urgent and contrary instructions. She hadn't really changed much; I recognized her instantly.

As I stared, Susie broke from the knot of people clustered in front of a store window and began striding purposefully toward me. My mouth opened, either in preparation to say something or to provide my brain with more oxygen, I don't know.

Susie never met my eyes, and I never spoke. She passed within ten feet of me, and I was paralyzed, unable to speak a single word. I turned as she walked by and watched her until the crowd swallowed her up. I've never seen her since.

Whatever I left back at Teen Town is apparently still there.

WHEN MEN TACKLE ROMANCE ON THEIR OWN

I don't know how women do it, but when men are confronted with a crisis and need to call upon their best friends to help them through it, they go into a huddle. A huddle is a small circle of men with everyone participating in listening to the quarterback tell them what the coach said to do. Sometimes they'll offer support to individual players, too, like "Bruce, try not to fall down this time," stuff like that.

Of course, if there's no coach and no quarterback, the men will huddle up and try thinking for themselves. This doesn't work as well.

When my friend Tom told me he was having a crisis in his marriage and wanted my help in solving it, I responded immediately. Tom told me he was inviting our neighbor Hurly into the huddle as well.

"Why?" I demanded, a little hurt. "I'm the Changed Man of the situation."

"Well, yeah, but Hurly is kind of a more sensitive guy than you are. And Hurly's wife Juliet is my Emily's best friend," Tom explained. "Besides . . ."

"Besides what?"

"Well, Hurly is happily married, and you're divorced."

From this I could only conclude that Tom was in such a state of distress it was interfering with his thinking process, so I decided not to argue further. More sensitive, ha! I suggested we convene this discussion at the local sports bar so that if the conversation about Tom's marital crisis got boring we could at least watch the game.

We settled into a booth so that we'd have some privacy. I secured the remote control and flipped through the channels while Tom bought a pitcher of beer.

Hurly leaned forward in classic male huddling behavior. "Tom, Juliet tells me you and Emily have been fighting."

"Well, I wouldn't call it fighting, exactly," Tom replied uncomfortably.

"Would you guys rather watch the basketball game or car crashes?" I interjected.

"Juliet says you've been kicked out of the house," Hurly prodded.

"Not completely out of the house," Tom objected. "I'm still allowed to sleep in the garage."

"Oh, it's *classic* car crashes," I clarified.

Hurly took a sip of his beer. "Why don't you tell us what happened?"

I joined the huddle, leaving the car crash channel muted out of respect for Tom having to sleep in the garage. In a nutshell, Emily had suddenly gotten furious for no reason at all, thought she did at some point mention Tom had forgotten their anniversary. And, as these things sometimes do, Emily's pique escalated into a whole series of accusations. Tom was thoughtless. He was unappreciative. He was unromantic.

"She says it seems like I don't think our relationship is important," Tom continued mournfully. "Hey, did you see that bus crash? Turn up the volume a second!"

"Hang on, Tom. Can you see the irony in what you just said? Think of your priorities! I'm sure that if Emily were here she'd tell you that you don't need the sound on to enjoy a bus crash," I countered.

"But . . ."

"Tom," Hurly asked quietly, "what sort of things do you do to make Emily feel special and appreciated?"

Tom looked at Hurly blankly.

"Hey, Hurly, you're being a little rough on Tom here, don't you think? I mean, what do you do, that makes Juliet feel special?"

"Oh. Well, a lot of times, if she's been working late, I'll have dinner ready for her when she gets home," Hurly mused.

"Hurly, have you ever tasted Tom's cooking? That wouldn't be thoughtful, that would be food poisoning."

"I could give her a list of my favorite meals," Tom suggested eagerly.

"Somehow, I think Emily's looking for something else," I told him.

"When I know she's been on her feet all day, I'll give Juliet a foot rub," Hurly continued.

Tom snorted. "Why would she be on her feet? She's the mayor, Hurly."

"Wait a minute Tom, I think Hurly's got something here. You rub her feet? How do you do that?"

"Yeah, like is she still standing, or what?" Tom added.

Hurly shook his head. "When she comes home, I sit with her on the couch and take her feet into my lap. I remove her shoes and put some massage oil in my hand and rub it into her toes, the arches of her feet, and up her calves."

There was a long silence.

"Whoa, really?" Tom finally said.

"Tom, that's what you should do," I decided authoritatively. "Emily's on her feet some of the day, right?"

"She's a nurse," Tom affirmed.

"Well, hey then! Just get some massage oil and rub her feet next time she's working late," I instructed.

Hurly nodded.

"Massage oil . . . would Crisco work?" Tom wanted to know.

I didn't talk to Tom for a few days, and then he called me at home one evening.

"Guess where I slept last night," he greeted me.

I paused. This was the most unexpected question I could ever recall him asking me.

"The garage!" he said happily. "In the bass boat!"

"Really? I thought you were going to try the foot rub thing."

"I did. That's why I slept in the bass boat, I was out there messing around with the fish finder and Emily came out with a bottle of wine . . . It's unbelievable. All I had to do was rub her feet!"

"There's something wrong with the fish finder?" I demanded.

"That Hurly is a genius. It's been fantastic."

"What do you mean, 'Hurly'? I was the one who told you to do it, he was just the person who brought up the topic, is all."

Tom apologized and said he had to go, he and Emily were planning a candlelit dinner. I hung up and thought about how seemingly simple it had been for Tom to infuse a little romance into his marriage. But who on earth would have thought of a foot rub?

THE PROBLEM IS EDUCATION, NOT MOTIVATION

As a Changed Man, I can assure you men don't understand this whole courtship thing. Yet what are we to make of these mysterious creatures, these women, who can captivate us from across the room simply by brushing the hair away from their faces? How can we possibly hope to take part in a game in which the rules are unpublished and the players are these fabulous beings who can cause all the air to leave our lungs by looking us in the eyes?

When relationships become more stable, when they are committed and long-term, men stop being romantic because part of their brain is saying, "Thank God that's over." Not because we're lazy, not because we take women for granted, but because courtship always makes us *afraid*.

Tom was lucky: He had someone like Hurly who had the idea of massaging Emily's feet and, more importantly, a Changed Man like myself to suggest Tom give it a try. And Sarah's problem with Doug was fixed when she asked me to intervene on her behalf. (Well, not really. As far as I am concerned, Sarah's problem isn't with Doug, it *is* Doug.) Most women don't have easy access to a Changed Man for help, so they're probably going to have to make the suggestion themselves. And by suggestion, I mean instruction.

But which would you rather have, a man who spontaneously forgets to be romantic, or a man who gives you foot rubs?

12.

— — —

THE THRONE

Why Men Spend the
Largest Amount of Time in the
Smallest Room in the House

It is as convenient and practical for a man and woman to share a bathroom as it is for them to share the same strand of dental floss; whether they do it simultaneously or sequentially, at least one of the two people is going to be less happy with the experience.

For the man, a bathroom is a place for contemplation. There's a very famous sculpture by a guy named Rodin that depicts a man in the bathroom, deep in thought, probably wondering where he put his magazine. You can tell by looking at him that the guy is not expending very much mental energy on his immediate surroundings. Everything a man does in a bathroom takes all of his concentration, and he doesn't waste any brain power on how the place is decorated, or whether everything is picked up and put away.

The difference between the way men and women regard the

bathroom is well illustrated at the health club. I've been told that women's locker rooms are fairly luxurious: they have individual showers, doors on the lavatories, and places to hang towels. Over on the men's side, showers are taken in an open room that resembles a delousing station. Water leaks out of rusty pipes, and the drains are clogged with bars of soap—if a man drops the soap in the shower, he never picks it up. The walls look like they're molting.

"You mean all the men are in one big . . . corral?" Sarah challenged me when I told her about it. Her look was utterly disbelieving. "Women would never put up with that!"

"I just tricked you into using the language that defines this whole issue!" I announced triumphantly.

"You tricked me? Oh, please do go on," she urged. "I have to hear more."

"This whole thing is about tolerance. When it comes to bathrooms, men are just more tolerant than women," I explained. "So when you said, 'never put up with,' you were saying, 'women are intolerant.'"

"So women are intolerant," Sarah mused.

"Exactly."

"And men are intolerable."

"Yes! What?"

"Yes, you are such a master trickster," she admired, batting her eyes at me.

"I didn't say that men are intolerable," I objected.

"But why is it such a big deal to men to prove they can have bad manners?" Sarah wanted to know. "Why do they have to leave the toilet seat up, and why can't they ever replace the toilet paper roll? Would it kill you to be just a little considerate?"

"Yes, it would kill me," I answered seriously.

"So you're saying that you want to be a Changed Man, but not if it means being nice."

I just hated it when Sarah framed the issue like this, because it made it difficult to cling stubbornly to my beliefs. Apparently I had been so tricky in my argument, she couldn't see my side, either, which is that when it comes to bathrooms, men and women will never agree.

AN ISSUE OF WIDE-RANGING, EARTH-SHATTERING IMPLICATIONS

One of the less endearing qualities of men is their willingness to argue heatedly and even endlessly about a subject they don't even care about. Case in point: The proper position of the toilet seat when not in use (most men won't dispute the proper position of the seat when it is being used).

I have spent hours and hours listening to men come to near blows debating such things as "Can you tell if a woman wants to have sex with you by her smell?" and "Resolved: If you're going to puke it's better to do it after margaritas than martinis." Yet never once have I heard a single mention of toilet seats. Trust me: Men don't talk about it, and they don't care about it.

Raise the subject with them, however, and they'll act as if you've come out in favor of a national movement to ban football. A man's brain frames the debate thusly: "Resolved: If we're leaving the toilet seat up we must have a good reason."

To gain some insight into the unreasonable nature of men on this whole controversy, I called my mother, who has claimed for fifty years that she lives with an unreasonable man.

"What is it that Dad says about leaving the toilet seat up that you suspect might be unreasonable?" I asked her delicately.

"It's not the seat, it's the lid," she responded.

"What?"

"It's the lid. He won't put the lid down."

"But it's the seat you care about," I informed her.

"No, so what about the seat? I want him to put the lid down."

"I'm pretty sure that's not right, Mom," I told her reluctantly. "Most of the women I know say it is the seat."

"Well, they're wrong."

I called my sister the doctor. "I just had the weirdest conversation with your mother."

"Now there's a surprise."

"I was asking her about why Dad won't put the toilet lid down . . ."

"It's the seat," she interrupted.

"Look, I'm not going to be able to be a Changed Man on this topic if women can't even agree what it is."

This was not turning out the way I had anticipated. I complained to Sarah at work. "I was going to find out what the unreasonable arguments are for keeping the seat up, and then explain the reasonable ones, and that's how I would be a Changed Man," I explained. "But the lid people say the seat people are wrong."

Sarah was gazing at me in a way that I've come to believe means she is impressed with my intellect. "The reasonable arguments," she repeated.

"Sure."

"Why don't you try these reasonable arguments out on me."

"Well, are you a lid person, or a seat person? Apparently it makes a huge difference."

"Let's put off that one for a minute, and just go with the arguments."

"Okay." I took a deep breath. "Well, for one thing, it is just as hard for a man to bend over in the middle of the night to check to see if a seat is down as it is for a woman."

"You're right!" Sarah beamed.

"I am? Well yeah, of course, I am," I responded. "And men sometimes have to sit down themselves, but you never hear them complaining."

"Right again!"

"And men use bathrooms more often than women, and more often in the standing position. So it makes more sense to leave it up."

"Brilliant!" Sarah said. "Got any more?"

"Something tells me you're somehow being sarcastic, here."

"Not at all. I think you are right on every point."

"Well, do you have any arguments for why the seat should be left down?"

"Oh . . ." Sarah looked up at the ceiling for a minute. "Okay, suppose I told you that a woman I know went in to use the toilet, and her husband had left the seat up, so she wound up sitting down on the porcelain and her doctor said that due to her injuries, she couldn't have sex for six months."

"Did that really happen?" I gasped, shocked.

"No, but it made you think, didn't it?"

"Look," I said sternly, "I'm talking real scientific argument, not fabricated stuff. Can you think of anything to say on the subject that is pro leaving the seat or the lid down?"

"Yes. One word: 'please.'"

"Sorry?"

"Please. Please leave it down. You're right, everything you say is right. It's terribly hard on a man to have to lift the seat. Women should be more diligent. It probably causes an imbalance in the rotation of the earth. But still, I'm asking you please. If we're ever in a position where we are sharing a bathroom, please leave it down for me. Okay? You win, you make perfect sense, just do me this favor."

In the end, I agreed that I would leave the seat down for her, but I still didn't have any information on how to change a man so that he would give up his unreasonable arguments on the subject.

I wound up doing more research, and in the end produced a piece entitled "How to Remodel a Man So He Puts the Toilet Lid Down," which I included when I sent this chapter to my editor at St. Martin's. She wrote me back saying she liked it, but that I had the topic wrong: "It's not the lid, it's the seat."

I've posted "How to Remodel a Man So He Puts the Toilet Lid Down," to my Web site at www.wbrucecameron.com. Go to my home page and click on the button mysteriously labeled "The Lid." Only people who have read this book will know what that means.

And regardless of whether you are a seat person or a lid person, there's a way you can solve all your problems forever, and never have to argue about the subject again: It's called a urinal, and it can be purchased for as little as $200. They use a lot less water and there's no seat to worry about at all. As far as I am concerned, it's worth it just to put an end to the controversy.

WHEN THE SINK LOOKS LIKE IT NEEDS A SHAVE

Every morning for most of my adult life, I've leaned into the mirror and scraped off the outermost layer of my face. There was a brief period when I grew a beard, and even though I looked very handsome with it—despite what everyone else said—I eventually grew tired of it because it itched and because once I overheard people talking about me mentioning the words "homeless problem."

If you live with a man who shaves, he may be less than diligent about rinsing the result down the drain, figuring it was hard enough to go through the effort of running the razor up and down his cheeks, and in the spirit of cooperation it should be someone else's job to clean up the mess he made.

TIP If this happens to you, try the following:

1. After he has left the bathroom, put the stopper in the drain and fill the sink with water.
2. Take his usual drinking glass and use it to capture the scum floating on the surface of the water.
3. Set the glass where he usually finds it.
4. When he asks what the heck is floating around in his drinking water, innocently tell him you thought he must have been saving the whiskers for a purpose, so you set them aside for him.
5. If he still doesn't get it, start using coffee cups, plates, etc. If he asks you why you keep doing this even after he told you he was not saving his whiskers, for heaven's sake, look wide-eyed and tell him you "forgot." There's a real good chance this is exactly the reason he has been telling you for why he doesn't rinse out his whiskers, so you're even.

Eventually, he'll grow so sick of finding bits of his face lying around that he'll start depriving you of the opportunity to save them—he will "remember."

REPLACING THE TOILET PAPER ROLL

Men generally react to toilet paper depletion by either (a) not using the bathroom for that purpose until the roll has been replaced, or (b) hunting down a new roll and placing it in the *vicinity* of the toilet, sometimes even on top of the cardboard tube left behind by the old roll. The only time you'll see him interested in the subject at all is if a roll accidentally gets wet and swells up like a puffer fish. He'll spend hours "freeze-drying" and microwaving it, proudly presenting you with what appears to be a wad of papier-mâché. "Look, honey. I fixed it!"

In this incident lies a clue to male behavior: Men will replace the roll of toilet paper if it feels like some sort of project. Men love projects, it makes them feel . . . manly.

To remodel a man, show him the following list. He'll become excited by the prospect of using so many of his tools, perhaps even to the point of insisting that he is the only person in the house qualified to effect toilet paper roll replacement. He probably won't read the accompanying instructions, but they are provided here anyway so it will seem more like a real project to him.

THE MANLY-MAN'S TOILET PAPER ROLL REPLACEMENT MANLY PROJECT TOOL CHECKLIST

1. Gasoline-driven electric generator
2. Stud removal ratchet
3. Abrasive cleaning stick
4. Adjustable depth stop rod
5. Air compressor
6. Radar detector
7. 50 pounds light block and tackle
8. 3-D holographic imaging system
9. Defibrillator
10. Air-driven drywall screw gun
11. Pipe clamp
12. C-clamp
13. Spring clamp
14. Summer clamp
15. Analog multitester
16. A digital multitester if you don't have analog
17. Ball-peen hammer
18. Ball-peens to hammer with the ball-peen hammer
19. Band clamps
20. Rope clamps

21. Cherrystone clamps
22. Bricklayer's hammer
23. Sledgehammer
24. Armand hammer
25. Carbon monoxide detector
26. Male cow emission detector
27. Chuck key
28. Charles key
29. Clamp pad
30. Box-end wrench
31. Double open-end wrench
32. Triple axle wrench
33. Triple toe loop wrench
34. Thin head wrench
35. Fat head wrench
36. Torque wrench
37. Wicked wrench
38. ¼" to ⅝" marine-grade stainless steel worm gear hose clamp
39. ¼" to ⅝" army-grade stainless steel worm gear hose clamp
40. 12-gallon 5.0 HP wet/dry vacuum; 6.5 HP is better, 200 HP is best
41. Plug ejecting arbor system
42. Pocket tape measure
43. Pocket for pocket tape measure
44. Rotary rasp and file
45. Screw extractor bit
46. Lampshade on head bit
47. Scratch awl
48. Screech owl
49. Vernier dial caliper
50. Explosive head bolts

The Manly-Man's Toilet Paper Roll Replacement Manly Project Instructions for Men Only

Note: You are unlikely to have all of the above tools lying around, but that's no excuse not to change the toilet paper roll. You should go to the hardware store and purchase what you need.

STEP 1: Determine if the woman you are living with is a "paper-over" or a "paper-under" person. You may think it makes no difference, but oh does it. If she is a paper-over person, then you should start referring to paper-under as wrong. If she is a paper-under person, then paper-over is wrong. To really get into the spirit of things, you should learn to speak bitterly of those who do their paper wrong, regardless of whether it is over or under.

STEP 2: Determine if the bathroom was installed using the metric system or the American system. If it was installed using metric, you will not be able to replace the toilet paper roll. When you run out of toilet paper, buy a new house.

STEP 3: Measure the distance from the reservoir tank to the toilet paper bracket. This distance should allow you to reach out without looking and find the toilet paper. As you know, most of the things men do in the bathroom are done without looking. If the bracket is not within the proper distance, you will not be able to replace the toilet paper roll without effecting some changes to the basic structure of the bathroom, which is why you have the sledgehammer.

STEP 4: Be sure you've completely used every last shred of paper on the toilet paper roll! Even if there is only a thumbnail-sized piece of paper, you should leave replacement up to the next person. (If you had any doubts that these instructions were manly, they've been removed now.)

STEP 5: Open the bathroom cabinet and look for a replacement toilet paper roll. You won't be able to find one—they're more invisible than mayonnaise in the refrigerator. Yell for a woman to come find it for you. Note: If you're like most men, it usually won't have occurred to you to check on the supply before it is critically needed, if you get my drift. This can be sort of embarrassing, as you aren't exactly dressed to receive company. Fortunately, you're a man, so you have a magazine, and magazines are made of paper, so . . .

STEP 6: Ignore any protests from anyone reacting to the number of tools you've assembled. Hey, do they want you to do this, or not? There's a right tool for everything. Tell them, "Man is a tool-using animal."*

STEP 7: Use the calipers to lightly compress both ends of the spring-loaded toilet paper tube. Affix a pipe clamp and clamp pad to the tube. Using a rope cleat and rope clamp, attach the pipe clamp to the block and tackle, fire up the compressor via plug-in to the electric generator, and using no more than five pounds of lift, pull the tube assembly from the bracket.

STEP 8: Well, that was certainly a lot of work in that last step! You should not feel bad that your enthusiasm is flagging. Perhaps it is time to take a look at the big picture. Why is this whole process necessary? Because people are using toilet paper. And can we be sure that people are using appropriate amounts of toilet paper? How come this ran out when you were in the bathroom? Why can't you have a home theater system? Life is so unfair!

---

*Man is a tool-using animal.—Thomas Carlyle (1795–1881)
 Man, having discovered tools, ceased to evolve biologically.—Stuart Chase (1888–1985)
 Stuart Chase was not a manly-man.—W. Bruce Cameron (1960–)

STEP 9: There must be an alternative to this hassle. Why don't they sell toilet paper in giant rolls that only have to be replaced once a year? Look at what a mess you've got in the bathroom. It will be far less fun to put all the tools away than it was to get them out. It will probably take an hour or more, and who is going to thank you for that? For that matter, who is going to thank you for replacing the toilet paper roll in the first place? It seems like more and more, you are doing all the work around here!

STEP 10: Turns out that using the drywall screw gun is pretty fun. It's also practical: Before, the picture in the bathroom was hanging by a thin wire, which could easily have snapped with the application of sudden g-forces. Now the picture is bolted to the wall and will survive the next invasion.

STEP 11: Another good idea would be some sort of service that comes around once a week and replaces the toilet paper roll automatically. That way, you'd never run out, and it would probably be pretty cost effective.

STEP 12: Having failed to interest any of your friends in investing in your toilet paper replacement service company—of which you would be the president, but they could have an important job, too—it's time to get back to work and finish the task. Use the analog multitester to test multiple things, and the adjustable depth stop rod to adjust the depth at which you want to stop rods. Apply some torque with the torque wrench, and clamp the new toilet paper roll tube with the hose clamp. If you do a good job with this, you'll never have to repeat this operation, because the hose clamp will prevent anyone from removing any paper from the roll. Stick the stupid thing back on the bracket, or at least on top of the bracket, and see if you can find someone to help you clean up.

MEN WHO ARE WET

I do some of my best thinking in the shower, particularly if I can see the TV from in there. And I've never met a woman who has ever complained about her man taking a shower, particularly if he has been playing basketball all afternoon. The remodeling that women seem to want to do to a man usually centers on his use of towels.

Many years ago, when I first got married, the issue came up in this fashion.

WIFE:
Why do you leave your towels lying on the floor?

INNOCENT BRUCE:
I don't!

WIFE:
Yes, you do! Look, it's lying on the bathroom floor right now.

FACTUAL BRUCE:
Well, I hung the towel up when I was finished, I don't know, did you go in later and put it on the floor?

WIFE:
Why on earth would I do something like that?

WISE BRUCE:
Why indeed.

WIFE:
Just next time, please hang it up.

SCIENTIFIC BRUCE:
I'll bet I know what happened. With the water from my body weighing down the towel, it slipped off the towel rack and fell to the floor.

WIFE:

Oh that's crazy, how could that happen?

NOT WANTING TO SHOW OFF HOW SMART HE IS BRUCE:

Well, just take my word for it, it has to do with physics.

WIFE:

If you hang it up properly, it won't fall off.

OKAY, YOU ASKED FOR IT BRUCE:

What I guess you don't understand is that water will evaporate unevenly from the surface of the towel. This destabilizes the weight of the towel, which slides off of the towel bar like a rope around a pulley with a weight on one end.

WIFE:

Good grief.

MAGNANIMOUS IN VICTORY BRUCE:

Don't feel bad that you didn't know this; men have a more instinctual grasp for the physical sciences than women.

WIFE:

I'd be happy if you would just grasp the physical science of folding the towel instead of just wadding it up and trying to jam it on the towel rack.

PARTING SHOT BRUCE:

Folding the towel traps the moisture and exacerbates the problem.

You'd think that would have ended the matter, but she insisted on remodeling me on this issue. From that point forward, whenever a towel behaved in a way that I had proven scientifically was unavoidable due to the physical property of evaporating water, she removed it from the bathroom and took it to the laundry room. This meant that by the end of the week, the only towel left for me to dry off with was the one we used to clean the dog when it came in from a rainy day. So I wound up being covered with muddy, itchy dog hair all day at work, looking a little like a werewolf who was having trouble committing to his transformation.

"Why do you have to wash towels, anyway?" I stormed. "When I get out of the shower, I'm completely clean! The water I am wiping off my body is just water! It's the same exact stuff you use to rinse the towels after you wash them!"

"I wouldn't have to wash them as much if you would hang them up so that the physical properties of evaporating Bruce water wouldn't make them fall to the floor," she explained.

This is one of the most effective ways to change a man . . . turn his own arguments against him. It is frankly unpleasant, because it means accepting his theories at face value, so I don't recommend it as anything but a last resort—but it does work.

THE BEST WAY TO REMODEL A MAN—REMODEL YOUR HOUSE!

If everything I've suggested sounds like an awful lot of work, you might want to consider the most sensible alternative, which is to simply add a bathroom onto your house. It will only increase the value of the property, and then your man will have a place that is his. You never have to go in there, and you can even install a mailbox so that magazines can be delivered directly to the room.

It really is the best solution.

13.

THE MALE DIET

Teaching a Man to Feed Himself

Inside every little boy is a teenager waiting to happen. A teenage boy is very much like a tantrum-throwing two-year-old, except often he is bigger than you are. He'll grow several inches a year in spurts that are timed to occur just after you've purchased him new clothes.

These spurts must be fueled, and the fuel of choice is everything there is to eat in the house, every day. The problem with this, besides bankruptcy, is that when the teenage boy grows older, his body stops growing, but he still thinks he can eat as much as he wants. I am one of these former teenage boys, and I'm outraged that you can gain two pounds of fat by eating one pound of pizza! I know our scientists are busy concentrating on calculating the exact age of the universe—which I am sure will be very helpful to all of us once that gets figured out—but in the meantime it would be nice if they would spend a little time determining just how it is possible to gain more weight than you ate.

The focus on quantity means that men are less concerned with quality. Listen carefully to a man describing his favorite restaurant: He's much less likely to use the phrase "amusing béarnaise sauce" than "huge sandwiches."

Here is a simple test to see if a person has a male appetite and therefore needs to be remodeled:

Male Appetite Test

1. You are driving down the road and you hit a deer. When you get out of your automobile, you are overwhelmed with a feeling of:

   a. Anger over the damage to your car.
   b. Sadness at the death of such a beautiful animal.
   c. Free meat!

2. The single most important development in nutrition in the past hundred years was:

   a. Iodized salt.
   b. Pasteurized milk.
   c. Aerosol cheese.

3. You're out to eat at a restaurant, and because business is slow you find yourself chatting with the waitress a lot. When

(continued)

the check comes, you decide to leave a larger tip than would normally be the case. You are motivated to do this by:

a. Her attentiveness to your every need. With her hovering nearby, you lacked for nothing.
b. Her personal situation, which you came to know as she recounted her story. She is a single mother struggling to raise two children and go to school at the same time. You admire her ambition and drive.
c. Her breasts.

4. The book *The Jungle* by Upton Sinclair made you feel:

a. Saddened at the plight of the working class, toiling for a pittance under inhumane circumstances.
b. Sickened by the unsanitary conditions depicted at the Chicago slaughterhouses.
c. Hungry.

5. Any meal can be improved by:

a. A good bottle of wine.
b. Pleasant company.
c. Ketchup.

Scoring: If you answered "C" to any of these, you are probably a man, and therefore need to be remodeled.

ATTACKING REFRIGERATOR BLINDNESS

After a couple of years of cooking for myself, it recently occurred to me that most recipes are made of the same basic building blocks, which, for the purposes of explanation, I will call ingredients. Given enough of these ingredients, one can prepare an entire meal!

This sounds pretty elementary, but most men I know, when left to their own devices, believe that to have a successful dinner, the recipe should refer to an entrée that is either ready-made or takeout. For example, the idea that a lasagna is not always something that comes frozen in its own baking dish but can, in fact, be cooked from a recipe containing canned marinara sauce, precooked lasagna noodles, and lasagna cheese mix is a rather foreign concept to a lot of guys who would prefer to think that their primary contribution to the meal should be to eat it.

Men react to this complicated issue in different ways. Here, for example, is my father's recipe for a turkey sandwich.

1. Ask wife to make a turkey sandwich.
2. Ask wife where she put the mayonnaise.
3. Ask wife if there are any potato chips.

TIP⟩ The first step in changing a man so that he is capable of feeding himself is teaching him to locate and use these so-called ingredients. As he stands numbly in front of the open refrigerator, unable to see the jar of mayonnaise right there in front of him, you may despair that this is even possible. Even this has a solution: To remodel a man so that he doesn't see the open refrigerator as nothing more than a signal that he should shout for your help, try the following.

1. Make an inventory of all the items in the refrigerator, except the mayonnaise jar.
2. Remove them.

I do recognize that this particular solution implies that you'll stop using any refrigerated products except mayonnaise, which may strike you as too large a sacrifice. So another way to attack refrigerator blindness is to remember the lesson of chapter eight: Men are the hunters in a relationship, while women are the gatherers. Finding the mayonnaise feels like a gathering behavior, which means "to pick," or "to harvest." Plucking a jar from the refrigerator and picking an apple from a branch are very similar activities to the hunter, who would only feel good about harvesting an apple if he shot it out of the tree.

What you should do is make a sock puppet in the shape of a wildebeest or wild boar and put it over the jar of mayonnaise. Similarly adorn the mustard and the pickles, using different beasts for them. Then when he opens he refrigerator door, he's on a safari!*

EATING BY THE NUMBERS

Of course, it isn't just teaching a man to recognize the ingredients in the refrigerator, it is also a matter of which are the right ingredients, an issue into which medical professionals seem to have significant input.

My own doctor has become an ever more irritating factor in my life, full of annoying admonishments every time I go to see him. In general, he seems to be faulting me for getting older, though he

---

*You won't need to produce sock puppets for the beer cans. Oddly, even men who are afflicted with the worst possible case of refrigerator blindness can always locate the beer.

has yet to prescribe anything effective in reversing this trend. Instead, he pores over printouts, shaking his head.

"Your LDL cholesterol is too high," he warns, as if I have any influence over it.

Fortunately for me, I have no head for numbers, so when my doctor sister peremptorily demands to know the exact degree that my LDL is "too high," I truthfully can't remember. "Eight hundred?" I guess.

"Eight hundred?" she gasps.

"Eight?" I amend.

"Only eight?" she demands.

"Look, whatever it is, it's too high," I respond impatiently. "I need to go, I have a frozen pizza coming out of the oven."

"What toppings are on the pizza?"

The suspicion in her voice makes me pause. "Well, pepperoni," I allow.

"Take it off," she snaps.

"Sausage."

"That goes, too."

"Canadian bacon."

"You can't eat that."

"But how can it be bad for you? It's from *Canada*," I protest. "Those people live as long as they care to!"

"Anything else?"

I'm silent.

"Hello? What else?"

"Meatballs."

"Meatballs? Since when do you put meatballs on your pizza?"

"Well, excuse me but isn't pizza Italian? And what could be more Italian than meatballs?"

"Take them off."

"But then it's not pizza! It's just flat red bread with some cheese on it!"

"It's not double cheese, is it?"

"I hate you!"

Well, I'm sorry, I know she's my sister and I shouldn't hate her but she practically ruined my pizza. I ate a couple of pieces her way and they were horrible. But I did it, didn't I? So I should get some LDL credit for that. I ate about half the pizza with just cheese, and half the pizza unaltered except that I added the toppings I'd scraped off the first half. That side tasted *great.*

I completely didn't need my sister and my daughters to get together on this issue, but I guess I left my cholesterol printout lying around and my older daughter saw it, probably picked it up thinking it was something she should borrow for her apartment. She called my sister and read her the numbers, which is why I found myself facing a lynch mob when I walked in the door that evening. I was immediately convicted of not taking my diet seriously as soon as they saw the bucket of fried chicken I was carrying, even though they had no proof that I had been planning to eat any of it.

My sentence was swift and cruel. My younger daughter, who had changed her major again and was now going to be a nutritionist instead of a celestial landscape artist or rumba teacher for wayward women or whatever was the previous scheme, would prepare some simple, healthy, and what sounded like completely flavorless meals for me to eat. I was to record my dietary experience in a journal so that I could discuss my concerns with my sister, who was now all of a sudden acting like she was some big important doctor. And my teenage son, who was on break from school, was staying with me all week, so he could (a) monitor my adherence to my diet, (b) make his own comments in the journal ("Like when I collapse from hunger, he writes that down?" I asked churlishly), and (c) consume all the food that I would normally get to eat.

At the end of the week, my daughters, my son, and my sister convened to review the journal, which I handed over rather proudly.

MONDAY

Breakfast	Oatmeal
Lunch	Tuna on toast
Dinner	Salad with no-fat dressing. Olive oil on pasta with sun-dried tomatoes. Steamed asparagus.
Dad comments:	Not much of a meal. I'm a little hungry. I feel like this was *One Day in the Life of Ivan Denisovich**

They turned to my son. "Well," he coughed, "he put like five spoonfuls of brown sugar in his oatmeal. He had two pieces of toast with butter on it, a slice of cold 'meat glutton' pizza, and then some salted peanuts."

Everyone gaped at me in horror.

"The pizza was leftovers," I protested. "You didn't say I had to write down leftovers."

"You shouldn't eat all that red meat," my younger daughter sniffed. "I'm a vegetarian."

"Hey, what my kids eat is hardly relevant to my own diet!" I retorted.

"I don't know about lunch but after dinner he had, um"—my son messed around with his papers while I glared at him—"an ice cream sandwich, some more peanuts, and a bag of cookies."

"Hey! You ate some cookies, too!" I shouted. I pointed my finger triumphantly at my son. "This whole thing is suspect!"

"Is what your kids eat really relevant?" my younger daughter rejoined sweetly.

"It sure is!" I snapped.

---

*Alexander Solzhenitsyn, Knopf, November 1995. That I'm able to make such an esoteric literary reference when living on such an austere diet is an indication of how seriously I take my writing.

TUESDAY

Breakfast	Scrambled eggs with no bacon. Toast. Juice. Coffee. A normal American breakfast. We live in America!
Lunch	Lunch I had to eat a hotdog because I was on the run and there was this hotdog cart there. It's not my fault.
Dinner	Chinese chicken salad and some fruit and that's it.
Dad comments:	A very healthy dinner; I can practically feel my LDL dropping, whatever that is.

"You can't eat like that!" my older daughter scolded me. "Hotdogs? Do you even know what goes in hotdogs?"

"No, do you?" I challenged.

They all fell silent. Score another one for Dad!

WEDNESDAY

Breakfast	Some sort of healthy cereal that tasted terrible with skim milk, which tasted terrible.
Lunch	All I had to eat for lunch was a salad that my younger daughter thoughtfully dropped by instead of going to her classes.
Dinner	Even though I was starving I had a boneless, skinless, flavorless chicken breast on some kind of brown rice, steamed broccoli, and for dessert mixed fruit.
Dad comments:	I dare anybody to complain about this!

Everyone turned to look at my son as if he were Angela Lansbury. "Well, there were these Burger King wrappers in his car," he began.

"Dad!" my daughters shrieked in unison.

"That doesn't prove anything!" I snapped. "They were just wrappers."

"And I saw you at the doughnut shop that day, too," my son stated. "I was riding past and you were at the counter."

"Aha! But you didn't actually see me eating any doughnuts, did you?" I sneered.

"Well yeah, actually, I circled around and then saw you eating a doughnut."

"One doughnut," I repeated, so that no one would miss the significance.

"Out of a bag that looked like it had a lot more," he added unhelpfully.

"I think there should be a rule that if it isn't written in the journal, we can't talk about it."

"Well, I'd say this journal paints a portrait of a man with too much saturated fat in his diet," my sister interrupted unprofessionally. "You're going to have to change the way you eat, Bruce."

Everyone seemed to agree with this, though why I didn't get a vote wasn't explained. Then they speculated on how they might conspire to cause this dietary calamity, with the following results.

1. My older daughter could move back in with me, except she was a grown woman now living on her own, and besides I had bought stuff to replace what she had borrowed so we'd have two vacuum cleaners, two kitchen tables, two toasters, etc.

2. My younger daughter could move back in with me, except that I would have to buy her a car so she could get to class, and she wants an Audi.

3. My son could move in with me, which would help because he would eat all of my food before I could get to it. But he lives with his mother most of the time and would not be willing to switch schools, etc., just to save his father's life.

With that they reluctantly concluded they would have to turn over responsibility for my diet to me, of all people. I tried to look resigned, but I couldn't help exchanging a triumphant glance with my dog, who has always supported my meal selections.

"Just eat more healthy things, Dad," my younger daughter urged.

I'm in favor of any instruction that starts with "just eat more," so I joyously agreed. "Okay!"

As soon as everyone left, I ordered a pizza. I was starving!

WHAT DO WOMEN EAT?

The lunch hour is an extremely important component of the business day for successful organizations, in that it allows hard-working people an opportunity to get out of the office and go on job interviews.

For men, the noon break is a time for bonding together, for grouping with like-minded males. Accountants go out to lunch with other accountants and talk about the intricacies of the tax code. Computer programmers get together to discuss the future of object-oriented programming. Salesmen get together to drink.

Women, on the other hand, seem to recognize no class distinctions at lunchtime. Executives and supervisors team up with receptionists and clerks—what, men wonder as they watch these females troop out of the office together, can that group possibly have in common?

Women also approach the selection of the restaurant differently, picking a place known more for its salads than for, say, food.

Women want to know that what they are eating is nutritious and balanced, men want to know that it was once able to move under its own power.

"To be a remodeled man, you'll need to go somewhere for lunch that serves something besides meat sandwiches," Sarah advised me.

I considered her statement, concluding that my position on this issue was "no." But after a while, I had to admit I was curious.

"Okay," I told her a few days later, leaning into her cubicle.

She pushed away from her computer, regarding me inquisitively. "Okay? Okay, what?"

"Okay, as in, let's go out to lunch."

She cocked her head, grinning at me. "So that must mean you like my new haircut."

I could feel my face heat up for some reason. "What? No, this isn't a date or anything. We're just two coworkers going to lunch. I want to see where women eat. You're the one who is so gung ho on remodeling me."

"But one of the coworkers has a cute haircut," she insisted mischievously.

"Okay, sure," I surrendered. "Whatever."

"Sure what?"

"Sure, it's cute. Your haircut is cute. Want to go to lunch?"

"But not on a date."

"No! Not a date," I affirmed with agitation.

"Then what has my haircut got to do with it?" she asked innocently.

I let her drive because her car was parked in the slot nearest the handicapped parking nearest the door—the Employee of the Month space. "You won again? How come I never win?" I demanded as I buckled my seat belt.

"Oh, I have no idea," Sarah told me. "Where do you want to go for lunch?"

"Someplace feminine. With, like, lace doilies and fragile teacups."

Sarah laughed. "Is that what you think? Doilies? There aren't any doilies at restaurants. Tell you what, there's a new place a lot of the women are talking about, I think it will be perfect."

The Gentle Spoon was a tiny restaurant that smelled bad. We sat on uncomfortable wooden chairs and rested our elbows on a table that wobbled precariously. I glanced morosely around the place, which was filled with people who seemed to be in a trance. The waitress was dressed in a material that looked like recycled carpeting. "Have you ever been to the Gentle Spoon before?" she asked.

"You mean people actually come back?" I replied, earning me an elbow from Sarah.

"This is our first time."

"But we're not on a date," I added.

The waitress nodded, unsurprised to hear that Sarah and I weren't a couple. "Well, the Gentle Spoon came into being because the community needed a place free from suffering," she recited. "Our furniture is made from recycled materials. Our food came to us voluntarily—nothing was hunted, and we don't subject it to the stresses of cooking. Our only beverage is rainwater, served at room temperature. The menus are made from a papyrus that we chewed ourselves. Any questions?"

"Yes, why do you call yourself a restaurant?" I asked.

"Just give us a minute," Sarah told the waitress. As soon as the woman left, Sarah began giggling at my expression.

"They don't cook the food?" I demanded of her. "So when you're not in the mood to cook yourself a meal you come to a restaurant where the staff isn't in the mood, either?"

"There are lots of things you like, here," Sarah advised me, peering at the menu. "You can have a salad."

"With no dressing!"

"They have lemon juice," she replied.

"What? Lemon juice isn't salad dressing, it's . . . it's furniture polish. And look at this, they have carrots. I thought all the food was here voluntarily! You think the carrots crawled out of the ground themselves?"

"It's such a guy thing to do, to sit and complain instead of making the best of the situation and finding something on the menu to try."

"Wait, I know why we're here. Dud wouldn't bring you," I exclaimed.

A smile played at the corners of her mouth. "His name is not 'Dud,' it's Doug."

"But I'm right, aren't I?"

Sarah shrugged, sighing. "But you're willing to try. There's no changing Doug; if you can't shoot it, he won't eat it."

A change in her tone made me hesitate—I felt the banter sliding away, something more serious settling over us. Sarah lifted her dark eyes and met mine, and I knew she was feeling it, too. I sensed there was something she needed to talk about, something important, emotional—so I snatched up a menu.

"What are you going to eat?"

My meal consisted of apples and pears that had fallen from the tree, drizzled in the milk from lactating coconuts and presented on a bed of mildew. Dessert was tumbleweed sweetened with a packet of Equal that I found in my pocket. Open a Dunkin' Donuts across the street from this place and you'd make a million dollars.

I had only one question for Sarah as we got into her car. "Hey, Sarah."

She stopped, holding a hand to her forehead to shield her eyes from the sun.

"Did you really get a haircut?"

CHANGING MY DIET

I should have known that my sister wouldn't be satisfied with how satisfied I was with this whole cholesterol situation. Her next move, though, was so maliciously devious and underhanded I never would have seen it coming: She took my parents and me out to dinner.

We gathered around a table and scrutinized the menu, which contained several items of bovine extraction.

"I'm going to get a steak," my father announced immediately and with gusto.

"Oh . . . shhh," my mother whispered to him.

"What?" he demanded. "It's a secret? Do you think they're trying to hide it from the cows?"

"Just, you know." She nodded in my direction.

My father frowned at me as if unsure of who I was.

"Bruce can't eat red meat," my sister explained unnecessarily and inaccurately.

"Too much red meat," I correctly primly.

"And a steak is too much," she rejoined smoothly.

My mother clapped her hands together. "You two have so much fun."

"Kansas City strip. I can also have clams as an appetizer," I countered defiantly.

"Not with drawn butter," she fired back.

"Clams sound great!" my father enthused. "But wouldn't you rather have them fried?"

"Bruce, what your sister is saying is that you need me to help you control your diet," my mother interjected.

I was stunned by this. Processing an instant recall of the evening's conversation thus far, I could find nothing that suggested my sister was saying anything even remotely like this, yet the two of them were regarding me with complete serenity.

"You should have the poached salmon," my mother decided. She turned to my sister. "Right?"

My sister nodded, and my mother gazed at me triumphantly.

"French fries," my father decided.

"Brown rice. Steamed," my mother beamed.

"Stop. This is crazy."

"Your sister told me I could make my tuna casserole recipe with no-fat soup and whole wheat pasta," my mother gushed. "I'm going to make one and take it to you on Monday. You'll feel better."

"Feel better? I'm not sick, Mom!"

My sister was watching me with merry eyes. Growing up, the children always considered my mother's tuna noodle casserole the gastronomical equivalent of weapons of mass destruction. We used to hand so much of it under the table to our canine it gained too much weight and we had to get a second dog.

"If you get the steak, they do this thing here with a scoop of garlic butter on top. You wouldn't believe it," my father confided to me.

"I'm having the salmon. Poached. Steamed brown rice. Raw carrots," I choked.

My father raised his eyebrows in surprise. "What? Why?"

"Because I'm watching my cholesterol," I stated in deadly serious tones. My mother sighed in contentment, and my sister just grinned.

MEN MAKE BETTER COOKS
THAN ANYBODY EXCEPT WOMEN

Males are fond of pointing out that "All the great chefs are men." Supposing for a moment that this is even true, it can also be said that "All the great National Football League quarterbacks are men." If you think this means that the average man is a great cook, then you know nothing about football.

I do prepare my own meals, but I don't pretend I'm about to be given a cooking show anytime soon. I've also adjusted my recipes to make them less likely to cause my mother's tuna noodles.

Here is my low-fat, low-cholesterol dinner for four, designed for a man with blood like mine.

INGREDIENTS

4 chicken breasts from chickens with no skin or bones

1 cup no-fat lime marinade

Lettuce, tomato, carrots, cucumbers—stuff like that for salad

1 onion

6 potatoes

4 ears of corn

1 large can of no-fat vegetarian baked beans (As if beans could be something other than vegetarian. Carnivorous baked beans? Come on.)

PREPARATION

1. About ten minutes before anyone shows up, yell "Oh my God I forgot to marinate the chicken breasts!" Pull them out of the freezer, dump them in a shallow dish, and spray the lime marinade all over them.

2. Five minutes later, check to verify they are still rock hard. In fact, the marinade appears to be freezing.

3. Put the whole assembly in the microwave and turn it on.
   - If you are using a glass pan, turn the chicken breasts after five minutes.
   - If you are using a metal pan, call the appliance repair guy and maybe the fire department.

4. Light the grill. Your guests will arrive and will need to be given beer. This should delay your next check of the chicken breasts, so that when you look at them again, they are all knobby and white in some areas and still frozen in others. You should probably have a beer yourself, now. It helps.

5. The salad is the easy part: Being a man, you either have a salad shooter or a food processor. I own a food processor, so I always turn the salad into a paste that has the consistency of baby food. My neighbor Tom has a salad shooter. He can fire cucumbers nine feet, landing about one in ten shots in the salad bowl. His wife Emily won't let him use it.

6. Put the chicken on the grill.

7. Use the food processor on the onion to turn into mulch and put it into a pan. Cut up the potatoes and put them on top of the onion paste, and turn on the burner.

8. Notice that your grill is filling the air with billowing clouds of smoke. Run screaming outside and open the cover. Grab your beer and dump it on the fire, turning the flames into a blast of steam.

9. Check on your guests, explaining that your recipe for chicken has a "beer basting." They are all regarding you oddly. A quick glance in the mirror reveals your face and body are stippled with black dots and you no longer have any eyebrows.

10. Back in the kitchen, you'll discover that the onions are completely adhered to the pan. It's as if they have decided to abandon being food in favor of becoming cookware. Poke at the mess with a spatula.

11. The chicken has shaken off the beer bath and is back to going pyrotechnic. Splash it with more beer.

12. Con one of your guests into shucking the corn.
13. Put a big pot of water on the stove. Chip at the potatoes some more, if it makes you feel any better.
14. Almost ready. Yell "Oh my God I forgot the beans!" and put them in an uncovered glass bowl in the microwave.
15. Collect the corn and dump it in the pot. Test the water— it's as if you're trying to punish the ears of corn by giving them a cold bath.
16. The sound of gunfire attracts your attention. The beans have gone to war against the inside of your microwave.
17. Get the chicken breasts. If you leave them outside for a few minutes, they won't set off the smoke alarm. Don't worry about your dog stealing them—he doesn't recognize them as food.
18. Serve dinner. This is not only a low-cholesterol meal, it is actually low-calorie as well, because nobody will seem to be hungry.
19. The corn will be ready in time for dessert.

THE TRADE-OFFS

You probably can see the problem: If you are worried about the health of your man, teaching him to recognize the location of various ingredients in your kitchen so that he can prepare a meal without involving you may actually work against your concerns. For example, Tom really can't cook anything. He grills ribs by slathering them with a sauce Emily concocts for him and then pulls them off the fire when she tells him they look ready. This is his recipe for ribs, and I'm willing to go along with the charade as long as he keeps inviting me to eat. His recipe for everything else is to ask Emily what she's cooking. So when Tom's doctor indicated that his blood was so thick with cholesterol it could be used to glue wood together, Emily was able to switch Tom to a fat-free, taste-free diet within twenty-four hours.

"Sometimes all we have is a salad," Tom whines. "Having nothing but salad for dinner is like raising a dog who can't bark at the moon."

I'm still trying to figure out what this means.

Our neighbor Hurly, on the other hand, loves to cook. He has a recipe for shrimp that is so rich in butter and fat and cream that every bite causes me to moan out loud with pleasure. His wife Juliet is more than a little concerned about his eating—and, for that matter, the fact that her husband and I are in the kitchen doing all this passionate moaning—but what can she do? Hurly knows how to cook. His dogs bark, Tom might say, and her ability to control Hurly's eating has been surrendered to the man because he knows how to feed himself.

Before you busy yourself making sock puppets, you should consider that remodeling a man so he can feed himself means you won't have any dogs who can't bark at your house anymore. It is only the man with the healthy heart who watches the moon rise in the silence of the dogs.

I think that's what it means, anyway.

14.

- - -

CULTURE

Taking Your Man Out in Public

Most women I know have a fondness for at least one of the arts—opera, ballet, poetry, and so on—while most men, if given a choice, prefer helicopter crashes. Showing the chopper crash in slow motion doesn't seem to enhance its feminine appeal—even if the movie reviewer spoke glowingly of the "balletlike violence." So remodeling a man starts off with a distinct problem when it comes to his culture: Men *do* appreciate culture, just not the same one as women. Women, for example, consider one of the most significant cultural developments of the last century to be the invention of modern dance by Martha Graham. For men, it's when they switched Darrens on *Bewitched*.

Women will agree with the statement "Art is in the eye of the beholder," but then will go on to state that men can't be considered valid "beholders" if they're going to insist on decorating the fire-place mantel with a singing fish. Most men are reluctant to accompany women to the opera or the ballet, because we're afraid we'll be expected to watch the thing. (I've been told that in the musical *Miss Saigon* there's actually a full-sized helicopter, but I'm not going to the performance unless someone can verify for me that it crashes.) It's not that we can't appreciate the fine arts, it is just that we are afraid our comas might be irreversible. It's more exciting to watch mold grow in the shower than to take in one of these highbrow events. Indeed, isn't a culture where you grow things like mold?

If you want your man to develop a more sophisticated appreciation of culture, start slowly, getting him used to it the way medieval knights used to build up immunity to deadly poisons by exposing themselves to it a little at a time.

FIRST STEP: ROMANTIC MOVIES

Men normally will go to the movies as long as they are convinced there will be some sort of plot. Take for example *For the Love of the Game*, based on the novel by Michael Shaara. Scores of men have willingly watched this chick flick, even though the baseball segments are interspersed with really boring filler subplots about some relationship with a woman who is totally beside the point of the picture. True, we've been burned enough with difficult-to-stomach elements like subtitles, black-and-white photography, and Julia Roberts to know that the medium of motion pictures can be used to terrible effect, but we'll keep going back to the theater with you and can eventually get used to being so soddenly bored.

Okay, if you're a woman reading this, you're probably starting to get worked up over my caustic references—in which case, my ploy worked perfectly. My highly psychological trick was necessary to demonstrate to you that it's not enough to drag your man to some plotless romantic comedy. You also want him to be able to speak politely and without disparagement, or you truly haven't remodeled your man. If your man has been embarrassing to you in front of your friends with his snide and tacky remarks, give him the following remodeled man's cheat sheet for polite conversation about romantic movies, and tell him to study it.

A CHANGED MAN'S CHEAT SHEET
TO BORING MOVIES

MOVIE	"PLOT" POINTS
Sabrina	Humphrey Bogart is running a big company that buys and sells continents. He is eighty years old, and steals the seventeen-year-old girlfriend from William Holden, who is fifty years old. It's a story about how love conquers all, even before the invention of Viagra.
Sleepless in Seattle	Hard to believe that anyone could be sleepless in this snoozer, but it is a good one to talk about because you simultaneously get credit for *An Affair to Remember,* to which countless references are made throughout the film. Meg Ryan and Tom Hanks fall in love with each other on the radio, then across a busy highway, and then on top of some building. It's about how love conquers all, even in the face of insomnia.
An Officer and a Gentleman	This is not the film where Julia Roberts plays a hooker, it's the one where Debra Winger plays the gold digger. Richard Gere plays the same guy he always does, which is to say, Mr. Ridiculously Handsome. You think with the title it is going to be a war movie, but ultimately they never get out of boot camp, which is sort of like a vampire movie that takes place entirely during

(continued)

WHAT TO SAY	WHAT NOT TO SAY

"Audrey Hepburn looked" (pick one):
   a) "marvelous"
   b) "fabulous"
   c) "stunningly prepubescent"
	"Humphrey Bogart looked like Bob Dole in this movie."

"I loved the ending of this movie!"	"I loved it when this movie finally ended!"
"Debra Winger is entirely convincing as a woman determined to use her beauty and wit to rescue her from her economic rut, only to realize that what really matters in life is to set aside such material considerations and marry a man strictly for love who	"How come Richard Gere went after Debra Winger and not the hot blonde with the big knockers?"

(continued)

A CHANGED MAN'S CHEAT SHEET
TO BORING MOVIES (continued)

MOVIE	"PLOT" POINTS
	the day. The only time they get to leave the base is to go to *prom*. Ultimately it is a story about how love conquers all, even when the male lead has a face like a department store mannequin.
Four Weddings and a Funeral	Hard to find something good to say about a movie so full of weddings you find yourself looking forward to a *funeral*. Here's the bottom line: It stars Hugh Grant, for whom the word "fop" was invented. Three quarters of the way through you find yourself actually sort of missing Richard Gere. It's a story about how love conquers all, though it doesn't seem to do much to help the guy in the funeral.
Sense and Sensibility	This is one of a whole series of movies based on the books by Jane Austin, wife of Six Million Dollar Man Steve Austin. All you need to know about Jane Austin flicks is that (a) the women keep passing out for some reason, apparently from romance or perhaps corset abuse, and (b) in every film there is a moment where the tension supposedly builds between a man and a woman over whether something is going to happen. (It doesn't.) This is a bit like watching two turtles narrowly avoid a collision. Ultimately, it is a story of how love conquers all, even lack of plot.

WHAT TO SAY	WHAT NOT TO SAY
can rescue her from her economic rut."	
"No one can play a callow idiot like Hugh Grant. He was born for this role!"	"In real life, someone would have shot Hugh Grant by the third wedding." (Which, I guess, would have made the funeral come earlier in the film.)
"Jane Austin wrote about universal themes of love and the economies of the heart. She revealed that issues of life that are so important today were played out exactly the same way two hundred years ago— only much, much more slowly."	"Remember the episode where Steve saved that family from being pinned under the burning truck?"

BEYOND MOVIES

Once you've got your man acclimated to talking about, and even going to, movies in which kissing is considered a valid replacement for gunfire, you're going to want him to take the next step. Don't make the mistake of trying to build on your successful campaign in an open and honest manner—such underhanded tactics will backfire.

> YOU:
>
> Since we've been to two Hugh Grant movies this month, I thought perhaps we could go to the opera.

> HIM:
>
> (emerging slowly from the sluggish, slothlike brain state the Hugh Grant films put him in) Uh ... huh? No! I thought since you've dragged me to two Hugh Grant movies, we could go to a monster truck rally!

TIP⟩ Of course, he doesn't really like monster truck rallies, he just wants to punish you for Hugh Grant. And, let's face it, *somebody* out there should be punished! So your persuasion techniques should focus on the exact opposite of punishment.

> YOU:
>
> Honey, the opera is in town, and I'd like us to go see it, but I have to buy some really exotic underwear for when we get home.

> HIM:
>
> I'll get the tickets!

REMODEL HIM SO YOU CAN
TAKE HIM OUT IN PUBLIC

Women often react to being out in social situations with their men the way teenagers react to being with their parents. If you're embarrassed by the things your man says, here is a list of cultural cues you can give him so that he can converse like the genteel gentleman you're trying to remodel him to be. Again, this first step is designed to provide him with polite comments to make instead of what he might come up with on his own. Then, as he finds himself drawn into conversations he would otherwise avoid, his natural male competitiveness (see chapter six) will cause him to want to win the discussion, and he'll be forced to start taking more of an interest in cultural events so that he'll know enough about what he's talking about to dominate the conversation.

These are Changed Man comments which I've tested in public, and reaction by women has generally been positive, or at least not negative. Not too negative, anyway.

Art

The correct name of the classic *Dogs Playing Poker* painting is *A Friend in Need*, painted by Cassius Coolidge. Calling it "Dogs Playing Poker" is a bit like calling the *Mona Lisa* "Woman Passing Gas."

Literature

The best book ever written in the history of the world is *8 Simple Rules for Dating My Teenage Daughter: And Other Tips from a Beleaguered Father (Not That Any of Them Work)* by W. Bruce Cameron.*

---

*Workman Publishing, New York, May 2001. Watching the TV show doesn't count as much as reading the book, though if all you do is buy the book, that's okay.

Plays

To Kill a Mockingbird: The closest they come to the title action is when they shoot a rabid dog.

The Iceman Commeth: No, he doesn'th.

Cat on a Hot Tin Roof: No cat. No roof.

Classical Music

Ludwig von Beethoven's middle name was not "Roll Over." (It's true, I looked it up.)

Ballet

Supposedly a lot of football players take ballet so they'll be more graceful as they slam their heads full force into the members of the other team. In ballet, a pirouette is a spin, a jeté is a jump, and a plié is a squat—all stuff that you can see in any typical NFL match up. In my opinion, instead of getting dressed up and going all the way downtown to see a ballet, it's a lot more convenient to sit in your living room and watch *Monday Night Football*. Plus, if you stay home, you can have beer all through the evening instead of trying to gulp it down during the three intermissions they give you in ballet.

Opera

If you can honestly say you enjoy opera, you are automatically given a pass for all other cultural events, since it is assumed that if you can sit through an opera, a ballet or a symphony would be a breeze. In the name of remodeling men everywhere, I sat through an opera called *Madame Butterfly,* and here are my notes. If you manage to get your man to go to an opera with you, give these to him so he'll know what the heck is going on. If you had your heart set on something other than *Madame Butterfly,* I'm sorry, but there's no way I'm doing another one.

A Changed Man's *Madame Butterfly*
Performance Notes

ACT I In opera, they sing everything, but it isn't like real singing because there's no song to it, just long, trembling yelling while music wanders around in the background. They actually sing stuff like "I'm exhausted" and "Would you prefer milk or lasagna?"

The play takes place in Japan, where apparently people are either (a) Japanese, or (b) white people with makeup in the corners of their eyes so they look *almost* Japanese. It opens with a real estate transaction. The main character, an American captain named B. F. Pinkerton, or "Big Fat Pinkerton" as I came to think of him, leases a dwelling from an agent who brokers in both real estate and wives, which must be a pretty difficult licensing exam. They actually sing the terms of the lease to each other, but it doesn't sound like a disclosure that would be legal in the state of California. The agent introduces B.F. to a servant whose name, I kid you not, is Fragrant Breath. Everyone seems to want to stay away from the guy.

Then we meet Madame Butterfly, for whom B.F. has ponied up a hundred yen—which as I write this is all of eighty-six cents—and let's just say the expression on B.F.'s face suggests he feels like he didn't get his money's worth.

In the course of talking to Madame Butterfly, everyone discovers that she is fifteen years old. This information stuns the American captain, who looks astounded that anyone so young could be so ugly. He thinks about it and decides he's going to marry her anyway, so naturally I figure that the plot will be the cops coming in to arrest the creep. This is when I still thought there was going to be a plot.

It is hard, actually, to get very worked up about the inappropriateness of the situation, since the woman is plainly not fifteen. In fact, the person she reminds me of is my elementary school teacher Mrs. Watson, who retired when I was in the third grade.

The ceremony itself is mercifully short—you could do thirty of them in the time it takes for one Catholic wedding. Basically, they kneel on the floor and drink out of ashtrays. Then B.F. makes everyone leave and his bride takes off her hat, revealing a hairstyle that resembles four black guinea pigs tied together with pink ribbons.

At this point you realize that they've been singing in Italian, even though they are all supposed to be Japanese!

Then, in a development similar to but ultimately completely unlike action, a guy dressed like Yoda storms in with a big stick and accuses her of turning her back on her people. She turns her back on him, and there is a moment of mild tension while everyone stares at each other, worried they might have accidentally made things interesting for the audience.

Yoda leaves, and I swear the new bride sings about insect mounting techniques. No one else in the audience laughs, though, so apparently this is the kind of thing they talk about at their houses as well.

The lights go down, they go to bed, the curtain closes, and for the first time in my life I'm in a theater fervently glad I haven't been shown any sex.

ACT II Three years have passed, which means this opera feels like it is happening in real time. The marriage broker shows up and wants Madame Butterfly to marry a rich guy named Yamadori. Apparently Captain B.F. Pinkerton is off sailing around on the USS *Abraham Lincoln* and hasn't bothered to make so much as a phone call to his teenage wife, which is all you need to do to get divorced in Japan.

I'm surprised that the American Bar Association hasn't boycotted this thing.

B.F. has sent a letter to Madame Butterfly explaining that now she is of legal age, he no longer finds her attractive. The guy sent to read it to her can't get past the first sentence, because Madame Butterfly keeps jumping up and singing about stones and rivers and electrical sockets, stuff like that. This woman practically in-vented attention deficit disorder.

Then the big surprise: In the three years that have passed, she's given birth to a nine-year-old son. Apparently in Japan, a year is about as worthless as a yen, and anybody can be whatever age he wants. So, the kid's five feet tall, but he's B.F.'s son from the night of the pierced insects. No one argues with the idea that the boy is supposed to be three years old, not even the kid, who doesn't know how to sing and thus is effectively rendered mute.

Rolling up a piece of paper like a telescope, Madame Butterfly announces that she sees her husband's ship in the harbor. Let me tell you, nothing makes you more proud to be an American than to hear a Japanese woman sing out the name Abraham Lincoln in Italian.

B.F. shows up with an American wife, and is bitterly disap-pointed that Madame Butterfly is not happy with the way things are turning out. He whines about how his whole day is ruined by this weepy broken-hearted woman. He was going to spend the af-ternoon playing golf, but now she's gone and upset him. Appar-ently he finds his own petulance to be very distressing.

In my opinion, B.F. is a waste of about three hundred pounds of human flesh.

Madame Butterfly says she'll let B.F. and his new bride take her son back to America with him, but only if B.F. will have the guts to meet her in person. Since B.F. is a cowardly bigamist, I'm betting he won't show.

Then, and I swear this is true, there is the operatic equivalent of the seventh-inning stretch. Guys come out and rake the sand smooth, and music is played while groundskeepers straighten stuff and put out some landscaping. Sadly, though, there is no beer man.

Next, Madame Butterfly stabs herself with a fan. Yes, a fan, one of those folding paper jobs. She keels over, the only person in the history of mankind to die from a paper cut.

And that's pretty much it. The curtain comes down, then goes back up, and everyone in the audience nods at each other as if they understood what just happened. The woman who played Madame Butterfly is given some flowers, and I was the only one who booed at Captain Pinkerton.

I'm not sorry I did, though. He was a B.F. loser.

A PLACE OF CULTURE

"So how would you like to experience a little more remodeling this weekend?" Sarah asked me casually as I labored over a column. I had decided to write about a snowball fight I'd had in grade school. After working for half an hour, I was off to a good start, having already written the words, "Snowball Fight in Grade School, by W. Bruce Cameron."

"Know any good snowball fight jokes?" I countered.

"There's this new exhibit at the art museum," she told me. "What are the chances you'd want to go with me tomorrow morning?"

"I'd say a snowball's chance in hell."

"Why? I thought you wanted to broaden your exposure to the arts," she reminded me.

"Something like that has the potential to really snowball out of control," I mused.

"Would you cut it out? Come on, when was the last time you went to the museum?"

"My son and I went to the carnivorous insect display a few years ago."

"I mean the *art* museum. How are you going to be a Changed Man if you've never even gone to an art museum?"

She had a point. I agreed to meet her the next morning out in front of the place. "So let me ask you a question. Suppose you were writing a column on snowball fights . . . what would you say?"

Sarah was standing on the marble steps when I arrived the next morning, and as I approached her, I noticed something different about her but couldn't figure out what it was. This is what women do to men all the time, they make some subtle change, like dying their hair or having their braces removed, and we're supposed to figure out what it is and mention it. Except plastic surgery, which we sometimes do spot—you're never supposed to bring that up.

I finally decided the change in Sarah was nothing more than her outfit, which around the office tended toward some kind of sweatpant thing and some kind of T-shirt thing. Today she was dressed in a pretty skirt and a sleeveless blouse. I was off the hook. I wouldn't have to mention anything if I didn't want to—clothing is optional, that way.

She sort of cocked her head as I approached. "What's the matter?"

"Huh? Oh, nothing."

"Why are you looking at me like that?" Her smile was puzzled.

"I guess I'm just trying to figure out what we're doing here when there's going to be a ball game today."

She laughed. "Okay, come on, let's get some remodeling done."

We went in to the exhibit, which had the cheerful title, "Angst, Despair, and Loss of Heart in Our Modern Life." This sounded like the sort of thing best viewed in haste, but I didn't notice that I was practically running across the marble floor until Sarah reached out and put her arm through mine. "We can slow down, I don't think they close for a couple of hours," she advised me lightly.

The first sculpture depicted a pile of what I, with my Changed Man appreciation of fine art, would classify as "stuff"—old radios, a refrigerator, a TV with no screen, and a couple of hand puppets shoved headfirst into a toaster. "I think what the artist is saying here is that he had a lot of junk in his garage," I mused. Sarah didn't laugh—maybe she had a bunch of junk in *her* garage. The next exhibit was a PC with a keyboard melted over the top of it like too much cheese on a pizza. "Some of those old computers ran really hot," I observed. Again, not much of a response from Sarah. It was my turn to be puzzled—she seemed preoccupied.

For the next couple of hours we walked from display to display, and at none of them did I absorb any culture—though I did learn some things about Sarah. All I could see was junk—stuff welded together and spray painted with no apparent pattern or approach whatsoever. One guy had nailed one hundred floppy disks to a white wall. That was it, just one hundred disks in a sort of high-tech checkerboard pattern. We stood and looked at that for fifteen minutes, which is something Sarah wanted to do. We just stood and stared at a rate of nine seconds per disk. I could have been in and out of the place in twenty minutes flat and seen everything in there, but Sarah liked to stop and ponder, cocking her head as if a bunch of floppy disks would appear different if you looked at them sideways. Our body languages argued with each other; mine saying, *Let's go,* hers saying, *Let's stand here,* and mine saying, *I'm so bored I'm hemorrhaging,* and hers saying, *We came here to look at this crap so let's hold still and look at it!* and mine saying, *Why didn't we go to the baseball game?* and hers saying, *You're kind of a jerk, you know that?*

At the far end of the exhibit, she glanced up at me and sighed. "You really aren't interested in this sort of thing, are you?"

"What sort of thing?" I replied innocently.

She gestured around the walls. "Cultural things."

"Ah. Well, I liked the one with the foot sticking up out of the garbage disposal."

"I love the art museum. When I was little, my dad always took me to the one near his office. He always knew how to cheer me up."

"If this is culture, then no, I don't like culture, I guess," I admitted reluctantly. We were now just sort of strolling aimlessly through the museum.

"Well . . ." Sarah murmured, sort of listlessly.

"Hey!" We'd entered a hall filled with old automobiles, each meticulously restored. "Wow, look at these!" I enthused.

Sarah remained standing at the threshold as I bent over the top of the velvet ropes and stared at the first vehicle. "It's a 'fifty-three Buick Skylark convertible," I marveled. "Look at the fit, the way the door is so seamlessly in the body. This thing was considered a compact, can you believe it?"

"It's huge," Sarah agreed, not moving.

"These wheels are practically like jewelry," I told her. "Chrome wire with knock-off hubs." I shook my head in admiration.

"I thought the fifties were all about fins," Sarah observed, coming to stand beside me.

"Oh, you want fins?" I responded. I showed her a 1959 Cadillac 62 series with tail fins larger than the Saturn V rocket. We strolled around among the autos and I pointed out things she might otherwise have missed, like the 3X2-barrel carbs on the 1964 GTO, the sheer audacity of the 1970 AMC AMX, the teardrop rear wheel wells on the legendary 'fifty-seven Chevy Bel Air.

"I never really considered any of this," she confessed. "I just thought of a car as a car. But you really . . . you really care about these vehicles from an *artistic* point of view, don't you?"

"Well, I like them better than a melted computer." We walked out into the sunshine. I did my best to hide my relief at leaving the "Depressing Modern Life" exhibit behind.

"Well, I'm glad that's over," I said.

We stopped. "I'm parked over there. I need to get going, I have yoga."

"You do yoga? Isn't that where you bend over and kiss the back of your head?"

"You should try it sometime," she replied distantly.

"You okay?"

"Listen, thanks for doing that. I just felt . . . I wanted to go to the art museum, and you're a good friend for coming." Her brown eyes searched my face, and I suddenly had an image of her as a little girl, finding solace in a building full of art stuff, wandering the halls with her father.

"What are you sad about?" I asked.

Sarah bit her lip. "Oh," she murmured weakly.

"Sarah?" I pulled her over to a bench and we sat down. "What is it?"

"Doug moved out. He's going back to Cleveland. There's a . . . he grew up there, and a girl he used to know, I guess he ran into her on a trip. Six months ago." Her eyes sparked bitterly. "Six months. How could I have been so stupid?"

"When did this happen?"

"Last week. I was trying to plan our vacation together, and he just blurts it out. Otherwise, I don't know when he would have told me."

I struggled with what to say to her. On the one hand, she was my friend, and I was sorry she was hurting. On the other, losing Doug was like having a giant wart removed—it was hard to come up with a sympathetic statement that didn't include the words "thank God!"

"Sarah, I'm sorry. Why didn't you say something earlier, so we could warn Cleveland?"

And then, to my dismay, Sarah started to cry.

"Hey, no, Sarah, I'm sorry, that was stupid. I'm . . . Hey, are you okay?"

"I guess I'm probably the worst person to ask about remodeling a man. What do I know? I thought the reason he was acting so secretive was because he was going to ask me to marry him!"

I held her against my shoulder and tried to figure out why someone like Sarah would even want to be married to someone like Doug, who had about as much personal appeal as a stuffed moose.

When Sarah recovered she apologized like crazy, of course, and I did my best to reassure her it was okay. She left to go to yoga, but

I lingered on the bench, my legs stretched out in the sun, feeling that I had sort of failed my friend. Changed as I was, I wasn't enough of a Changed Man to help Sarah. I kept running our conversation through my mind, and every time I rewrote the dialogue so that I managed to say something more appropriate, something to make her feel better.

"Time to warn Cleveland." Good grief. Sometimes I could be really dense.

MEN AND CULTURE:
NOT A GOOD FIT

I'm a man, so even though I am willing to watch an occasional bad movie or go to one opera in my life—which I've done, so thank God that's over with—I can only pretend to enjoy any of it.

To get a sense for how a man feels about cultural events, try this: Turn on the television. Find a show where two men are in a boat, fishing, and when one of them hooks a fish, the other guy says "That's a beauty," and then they hold the fish up for the camera and grin, and then they do the exact same thing again. Sit there and force yourself to watch men reeling in fish for an hour, even if you get urgent messages from your brain warning you of the potential for permanent damage. Remind yourself that this is just one episode of the show, and that every day there are hours and hours of this stuff being broadcast into homes, and maybe it is two different guys but it sure looks like it is the same fish every time. Then picture yourself watching this show while wearing really uncomfortable clothes, and you'll understand how men feel about culture.

If you still don't get it, you may actually have to go fishing. Try ice fishing, which is a bit like sitting and staring at a coffee can all day long. When it feels like the seat of your pants have gone glacier, say to yourself, "This is exactly how my man feels about culture."

The point of all this is that you won't understand how in the world men can spend their time fishing, or watching other men fishing on television—and men cannot understand how you can watch opera, or Hugh Grant. He'll never enjoy it—the best you can hope for is that once you've got him attending something cultural he won't embarrass you.

15.

- - -

CLOTHING

Many Men Dress with Style,
and That Style Is "Out Of"

When it comes to clothing, men will often settle into a particular style that they feel works for them, even though it may not work so well for other people. This explains why you can encounter a man you haven't seen in a decade and he appears to be dressed in exactly the same thing he was wearing ten years ago, though it can't possibly shed light on why he went with Hawaiian shirts in the first place. Men will also often stick with the same size, oblivious to the fact that while jeans still come in a size thirty-four, their stomachs don't. It usually falls to some poor woman to take on the sad duty of explaining to a man why it is that every time he puts on his new pants he gets cramps.

For a lot of males, this is the event that triggers the purchase of new clothing: The old clothes don't feel good anymore. Most of the time, left to their own devices, they'll simply go out and purchase stuff that pretty much duplicates what they already have.

Men often seem oblivious to fashion, or even how they look in various styles, which is far different from women. I have never heard one man turn to another and ask, "Do these jeans make my butt look fat?" I have, however, heard one say, "Geez, these stupid pants my wife bought me keep crawling up my crack!" Men care far more about how clothing makes them feel than how it makes them look.

Once a man has found something comfortable, he wants to put it on and wear it all weekend, rarely thinking anything is wrong with reaching out for where he threw it in the corner the night before, and shrugging back into it for another day. Men also simply cannot understand why one would want to stop wearing something simply because it has gotten old. Like my Aerosmith concert sweatshirt: what a historic event! Even though I didn't actually go to the concert and even though the garment is actually more "sweat" than "shirt," I still want to wear it on Saturday mornings. It has a lot of good memories, that sweatshirt, and I understand that the concert was great.

When I take off my Aerosmith sweatshirt and toss it at the laundry hamper, I am not saying, "I'm done with this, so I'm throwing it in front of the hamper." I'm saying, as I explained earlier, "I might, or might not, be through with this, so for now, it goes in front of the hamper." Besides, my hamper has a lid, so there is no way to throw dirty clothes at it and have them actually land inside.

Now I am a Changed Man, remodeled when it comes to letting my clothing reside by the hamper instead of in it. I blame my older daughter for this transformation. I had taken my sweatshirt and tossed it in front of the hamper with a perfect hook from across the room—had it been a basketball at buzzer time, the crowd would have been on its feet. There were, I admit, about four day's worth of great hook shots already on the floor when the Aerosmith shirt hit, but I was planning to scoop them all up and put them in the hamper on laundry day, so this wasn't unusual. What was unusual was that sometime during the night the cat my daughter gave me—over what I believe we've established for the record were my strenuous objections—went up to the pile of clothes and urinated on it!

"This stupid cat has been peeing on the sweatshirt I got at the Aerosmith concert!" I wailed to her.

"You still have that thing?" my older daughter demanded.

"It's my favorite sweatshirt," I thundered, "it memorializes one of the greatest concerts of all time, and Mittens ruined it."

"Well, just wash it, Dad," she advised impatiently.

"I am washing it, but you need to train this cat to stop doing that!"

"I don't think you can do that, Dad. Cats pee to establish the parts of their territory that contain clothes that are out of style."

"Very funny."

"Well, I think I have some good news for you. I finally found someone who might be willing to take Mittens. One of the women in the office was just telling me she was thinking of getting a kitten."

"What? Give her my cat? That's your solution to the problem you caused?

"You said . . ."

"I suppose you think that the first time you wet your diapers, we should have given you away to some woman from the office!" I fumed.

She laughed. "No, but Dad . . ."

"Never mind!" I slammed the phone down and picked up Mittens, kissing her on top of her adorable little head. "I can't believe she would even suggest such a thing," I told her.

THE SIXTH SENSE: STYLE

Clothing style has always mystified me, and I'm not just talking about leisure suits. I remember in junior high school, the popular girls always knew the exact day upon which it was proper to switch from the winter to the spring wardrobe. Anyone who switched a day early or a day late was thought to be completely out of touch, and those of us who never really switched at all were considered incapable of social interaction.

Part of the problem men have in dressing themselves is a lack of comprehension around what colors go with what other colors. This is complicated by all the new crayons for the Crayola box that have been invented since third-grade art class—colors like Heather. Heather is either purple or green, which is a concept that a man cannot possibly comprehend. A man is also unlikely to understand why his green pants shouldn't be worn with this green striped shirt—if green doesn't match green, what does it match?

In case your man is sartorially challenged, here is a handy table that will translate colors from names like Heather and provide helpful hints on what will match them. Post this inside his closet, where he can refer to it often.

A HELPFUL COLOR MATCHING TABLE

COLOR	MEANS	MATCHES
Taupe	Brown	Nothing
Eggplant	Purple	Nothing
Oatmeal	Brown	Nothing

(continued)

A HELPFUL COLOR MATCHING TABLE (continued)

COLOR	MEANS	MATCHES
Indigo	Blue	Nothing
Ecru	Brown	Nothing
Mustard	Yellow	Nothing
Fawn	Brown	Nothing
Mocha	Brown	Nothing
Brown	Brown	Nothing

SHOPPING WITH SARAH

When I told Sarah that I had been chosen by my fellow writers to speak at the annual meeting of the Society of Journalists Who Are Disappointed in Their Keynote Speaker, her immediate reaction was to attack me. Or rather, she attacked my clothing.

"We've got to get you a new wardrobe!" she announced, despite the fact that it seemed as though we had more or less agreed at the art exhibit that she should abandon any efforts to remodel me. She advised me that the next weekend she was dragging me to the mall for a shopping trip. This sounded about as much fun as getting together for a colonoscopy, but Sarah had been acting listless and morose, and this was the first sign of life I'd seen in her since Doug moved his putrid mass back to Cleveland. It might make her happy and I felt like I owed her something for having failed her on the steps of the museum. I decided to go and to keep my complaints to a minimum.

"I don't want to do this," I stated uncomplainingly on the day of the trip.

"We just have to do something about your clothing," she declared grimly as she drove. "I'm tired of seeing you in the same things you've been wearing since I met you."

"Hey, these are new socks," I pointed out.

She was silent for a moment. "Why do I smell cat urine?" she wondered, sniffing.

I ignored this.

"Like that sweatshirt you've got on. It's so old, the picture on it makes Steven Tyler look like Liv Tyler. When was the last time you wore it?"

"How am I supposed to remember something like that?" I snapped.

"Was it, I don't know and this could be a wild guess, yesterday?"

"Well . . . maybe."

"So you put on the same clothes you had on yesterday," she affirmed flatly, like a prosecutor repeating something for the jury.

"Hey, I gave them the sniff test," I protested.

"The sniff test? There is no sniff test. Why do men think there's a sniff test?"

"Well, how else can you tell if you can wear something?"

"I don't know, this might sound like a crazy theory, but maybe if it is clean?"

"Ha! But what if it was clean when you put it on, but you need to check to smell if your armpits are bad? You do this!" I demonstrated a very socially suave maneuver, gracefully lifting my arm and sliding my nose into the pit with a genteel motion.

"What's that?" she shouted. Sarah had been under a lot of stress and I was worried she might need psychiatric attention.

"You pretend to wipe your nose on your sleeve, but really what you are doing is checking your armpit," I responded smugly.

"Since when is it okay to wipe your nose on your sleeve? Are you completely crazy?" she raved.

See? It is a sign of psychiatric instability when the patient starts accusing everyone else of insanity.

We arrived at the mall and plunged into a clothing store. "I'm really getting tired of this," I told Sarah.

"We've been here five minutes," she responded. She summoned a saleswoman. "Do you have these in his size?" she wanted to know, holding up a pair of pants.

The woman snapped her gum. She was attractive, probably in her thirties. "What's his size?"

Sarah turned to me. "What's your size?" she translated.

I shrugged. "How the heck would I know?"

The two females exchanged a look. "Let me see," the salesclerk suggested. She reached out and put her hands in my pants. The unexpected sensation of a strange woman's fingers patting me on the butt caused me to blink in surprise. "Okay, let me see if we have these in stock."

Sarah shrugged. "If they don't have your size, let's move on."

"But I really like this store!" I objected.

They didn't have the right pants, so she dragged me out of there, even though I stated my willingness to have the salesclerk check my tag again, just to make sure.

"I have a better idea," Sarah told me.

"This is pointless," I complained. "Let's go look at digital televisions."

"You just bought a television!"

"Right, but that doesn't mean you stop looking at them," I explained sensibly.

"We're here to get you some new clothes," she proclaimed grimly. "You can look at televisions on your own time."

"You mean today is suddenly not my own time?"

Wanting to make this whole thing a success if for no other reason than to give Sarah something to be happy about, I dug a sweater out of the stacks and showed it to her.

It did not make her happy.

"That's what you picked out? You already have one just like it!"

"Well, isn't that proof that I like it, then?"

I brightened when we got back out into the mall. "Hey, let's go there!" I suggested, pointing.

She rolled her eyes, but reluctantly agreed to follow me into the logo apparel store, where I bought two shirts, a cap, and a pair of pants all emblazoned with the emblems of teams I admire.

Now, that's shopping!

AS YOU MAY HAVE NOTICED, THERE IS A DIFFERENCE BETWEEN MEN AND WOMEN

There's a word for men who like to dress up in pumps, pantyhose and tight skirts, and that word is "masochist." Otherwise, men put on clothing that is much more sensible and utilitarian.

"Men," I declared to my neighbors Hurly and Tom, "put on clothes for comfort. Women dress for style."

They nodded in general agreement. "Further," I went on to tell them, "men dress for themselves as individuals. Women, on the other hand, put on clothes to please groups of other women. What they themselves would like to wear, or even what men would like them to wear, isn't even considered."

There was a pause while our waitress—who was dressed in tight hot pants, high heels, and a tiny blouse with owl eyes on it—set a bowl of shriveled chicken wings on the table in front of us.

"The food here is great," Tom exulted gleefully. Hurly and I exchanged a skeptical glance. "My wife hates to come here, though."

"I can't imagine why," Hurly observed.

"Me, neither," Tom agreed, gnawing on a piece of chicken.

"So that's my Changed Man conclusion about all of this," I continued. "When it comes to clothing, men don't care what they look like, they only want to be comfortable."

Hurly cocked his head at me. "Maybe you should question your perspective, Bruce. It sounds like you expect that all men are essentially just like you. But really, we're all different, aren't we?"

I looked around the restaurant, which was being patronized exclusively by men—men who certainly weren't here for the menu. "We're probably more alike than you think, Hurly."

"But still, with your Changed Man campaign, it seems like you are making the assumption that every male needs to be changed from being like you," he reasoned.

"No, everyone needs to be changed *to* being like me," I countered. "That's what women want."

"I got to say, I go along with what Bruce is saying here, Hurly," Tom weighed in loyally. "This whole Changed Personality thing, it's a great scam."

"It's not a scam!" I snapped.

"But I'll bet the chicks really fall for it," Tom said slyly.

"There's nothing to fall for. I really am a Changed Man!"

"But really. When you talk about how men dress, you're talking about how *you* dress. You certainly aren't talking about me," Hurly insisted. "So if every man is unique, then it only stands to reason that some men need more changing than others, or perhaps it would be best to say, *different* changing from others."

"So you're saying my scientifically proven techniques for remodeling a man will only work on men who are just like me."

"Not exactly like you, but similar, more like you than like other guys," Hurly elaborated. "But I imagine there are a lot of guys like you, Bruce."

"If you really want to help men," Tom offered, "write a book on how to get our wives to dress like our waitress."

"Now *that* would be a good idea," Hurly agreed.

WHAT WORKS, WHAT DOESN'T

TIP › What Tom and Hurly revealed is that while there is some dis-
agreement among men over how they should dress, there seems to
be a fair amount of male unanimity about what women should
wear. This suggests that if you are unhappy with how your man
dresses, there's a fairly easy solution. Let's say he has a certain
sweatshirt that says "Aerosmith 1970 Nipmuc Regional High
School Concert, Mendon MA" across the front, and you're sick of
looking at it even though it references a classic moment in rock 'n'
roll history. Let's further say he doesn't have a pet cat like Mittens,
who is not a Steven Tyler fan and who will desecrate the shirt the
moment it is left out in the open. You could just throw the thing
out and be done with it, except you know that your man would tear
the entire house apart, swearing and moaning. He'll never accuse
you of anything directly but instead go on and on about how he
can't imagine what happened to that sweatshirt, it was a classic,
one-of-a-kind that if he has to go on eBay to replace it will cost
probably a thousand dollars, if he can even find one.

Instead, offer to trade. The issue, after all, is comfort. Tell him
that if he'll dress less comfortably, so will you. Show him some ex-
amples in lingerie catalogs of just how uncomfortable you're willing to be, keeping in mind that there's a restaurant in town where
men eat little pieces of fried chicken skin for no reason other than
the fact that the waitress is wearing an outfit that binds every inch
of her body.

Of course, it's easier if your man hates to shop. If he's not willing to go into a men's store to buy what he wants, he's rather at
your mercy, isn't he?

16.

— — —

MAKING A MAN MORE
SENSITIVE, SPIRITUAL,
AND IN TOUCH WITH HIMSELF

Even Though He Thinks It's "Girly"

As any dentist will tell you, men are actually very sensitive creatures. We just prefer to hide our feelings. For example, when my oldest child was born and I held her in my arms for the first time, my heart was full of love, and I felt like weeping with joy. I saved my tears, though, releasing them later, in private, when I saw the bill for her first prom dress.

It is usually difficult for a man to express out loud how he is feeling, unless he has just hit his thumb with a hammer. This means that when we do try to put our innermost thoughts into words, we usually fumble a little.

When I was a young boy, I was infatuated with a girl my age named Libby Lash. Her parents were good friends of our family, so we often took summer vacations together, meaning I would not only have exclusive access to her, but that I was additionally treated to a daily view of her in a bikini. At age twelve, this was pretty over-whelming. I struggled mightily with some way to express my feelings for her, which ranged from morose despair to nausea, but couldn't seem to stammer out a word.

One year our two families were all jammed into a small cottage for the fifth rainy day in a row, trying to think of indoor activities that didn't include multiple homicide. Libby baked cookies, which turned out to be such a big hit they were all eaten immediately. My mother purchased some replacements for Libby's treats, but the store just couldn't match, chocolate chunk for chocolate chunk, what Libby's homemade efforts had produced. I mentioned to my father how much better Libby's cookies tasted, and he advised me to tell her, which sent me into instant panic. Say something complimentary to a girl? Make myself vulnerable?

I think maybe my dad knew I had a crush on her, possibly because I had written "I love Libby" all over the inside of my top secret journal that I left lying around because I was too lazy to hide it. He gave me a Go-ahead-you-can-do-this sort of look, so I screwed up my manly courage and walked over to where Libby was reading a book.

"Hey Libby," I greeted her. I held up the store-bought dessert in a trembling hand. "These cookies are worse than yours!"*

As a man, I haven't improved much in my ability to deliver a disarming compliment. Asked one time by a woman if I thought she looked good in a new outfit, I told her, "Well, I sure like it better than anything else I've seen you in!" This flattering observation won me no points with her—to this day, she seems reluctant even to speak to me, which is sort of an odd relationship to have with one's therapist.

---

*My bold declaration did not succeed in winning her heart, but Libby, if you are out there reading this, I want you to know that I still, deep inside, harbor an enduring passion for your chocolate chip cookies. Naturally, I'm not seriously suggesting you forward me a recipe—that would be an imposition. So if you would just send the cookies themselves, I'd appreciate it.

This lack of sensitivity can even extend to a man's own children.

"Sometimes when I am alone in the library, I feel so isolated, like I don't have any friends in the world," my younger daughter told me during a break from college. "It's hard to focus when I feel so lonely."

I patted her on the shoulder. "Oh honey," I comforted, not mentioning the fact that whenever I saw her on campus, she seemed to be in the middle of a pack of about a dozen friends.

"Did you ever feel like that, Dad?"

I cocked my head, trying to remember if I ever went to the college library. Did my school even have a library? "Sometimes, I guess." Certainly if I was in the library, I would have been lonely; none of my fraternity brothers would have been there, that's for sure.

"What should I do?" she wanted to know.

As a man, the clear solution would seem to be to stay out of the library. However, as a Changed Man, I knew she needed more from me. "Have you talked to your mother about this?"

TOWARD A MORE SENSITIVE BRUCE

In my quest to become a Changed Man, I decided to venture into the heart of feminine ritual, to plunge into a snake pit of feelings, sentiments, and shared emotions. I would sit side by side with women as they conducted an ancient ceremony that spans the centuries and unifies women from all over the earth in one single, shared commonality. I would receive the sacrament. I would attend a baby shower.

Now, modern times have given vent to a modern shower, a couples event where men and women together celebrate the impending birth of a child, but this was different: My cousin Jen was being given what was shaping up to be a women-only shower, a party to which I was invited as a joke, because I was her number two, fallback-only-in-dire-emergency, birth coach. I surprised everyone by accepting the invitation. You can't remodel yourself if you aren't willing to take some risks.

The Baby Shower:
No Baby, No Shower

The baby shower for Jen was a surprise, which I found out when I called her and told her I wasn't sure I was going to be able to make it. When I realized that I had let the cat out of the bag, I recovered by stating, "Oh, sorry, I meant to call my other cousin Jen!" Then I pretended the phone connection was breaking up. "Oops, going through a tunnel."

That was a close one!

When I showed up at the party, there was considerable consternation over the fact that I was apparently a male. The theme of the party was "ladies high tea," and everyone came wearing a big stupid hat except me. There was, of course, tea, plus a dinner buffet consisting of the following:

Cookies

Chocolate cake

Ice cream

Sugar-coated candy

Lemon bars

Dessert

When Jen arrived, we all leaped out from hiding places, yelled "Surprise!" and knocked over the punch bowl. Well, okay, I was the only person to do this.

The women were very pleased that Jen was surprised, explaining how difficult it was to keep the party a secret from her for the several weeks of planning it took. As they said this, Jen smiled knowingly at me, no doubt reflecting on how cleverly I had misled her.

Once everyone had loaded up plates, we all went into the living room, the big stupid hats banging into each other as the women settled down. The leader of the group was named Loretta—it was her house we were sitting in and her sugar we were consuming. Loretta was about ten years older than Jen and had three children. She sat on the couch with two other women in hats, looking like the queen of the mushrooms.

"First, let's play the circumference game," Loretta gushed. Everyone seemed excited to do this. Loretta produced blue and pink balls of yarn, instructing us to snip off the amount of yarn we thought represented the circumference of Jen's waistline, which in my opinion was growing alarmingly large. If you thought the baby was going to be a boy, you were supposed to use the blue yarn, and if a girl, the pink. Apparently the attendees thought that once we'd voted Jen would have to go along with the majority.

Everyone laughed as the yarn was snipped. But as I glanced at Jen, I noticed her cheeks were burning red, a telltale sign of distress that I recognized from when she was a child. Loretta picked the pink skein, pulling off so much yarn she could have tied Pavarotti to a beanbag chair.

Well look, I might be a Changed Man, sensitive and caring, but some male part of me reacted to this. When Loretta stood with Jen and finally selected the closest match—my own cut turned out to be way too small, earning me a different sort of blush from my cousin—I stood also, picking up the winning yarn and slipping it around Loretta's own considerable girth. "Well hey, Loretta, it fits you, too!" I hooted mischievously. Several of the women tittered, so stoned on glucose and chocolate they couldn't see the steely look in Loretta's eye.

The battle thus joined, Loretta spent the rest of the evening perfecting the art of looking past me whenever she cast a glance in my direction, which suited me just fine. I didn't really see the need to talk to her again, until the topic of the evening turned to "How Much It Really Hurts to Have Children."

As you know, I am remodeled on this topic, so I didn't object when the assembled mothers all agreed that there is no experience more painful in the universe than giving birth, not even being eaten alive by sharks, not having a burning meteor hit you in the stomach, not listening to James Carville. Then they went into descriptions for which "excruciating detail" is an entirely apt characterization. Apparently every mother can remember every contraction she has ever had.

And there was more. Episiotomies, "nipple flake," breech births . . . I may not be as sensitive as women, but why would anyone tell an expectant mother these stories?

I caught sight of Jen's face as Loretta was describing the first time she went through the part of labor called "transition," which is when the process transitions from being merely unbearable to being truly excruciating. My brain started talking before my Changed Man perspective could censor myself.

"But in the end, you got a baby, right, Loretta?"

She paused, looking warily in my direction, though she still avoided my eyes.

"I mean, that's pretty special, right? Your son was born, as a result of all this."

"Well, of course," she acknowledged.

"And then you went through it two more times, right? I mean, I know it hurt, but it was worth it to have your children, don't you think?"

Loretta nodded. "I love my children," she replied, meaning, *I really hate Bruce Cameron.* She was so angry her lips were trembling, causing powdered sugar to fall into her lap in a light sprinkle.

"Okay then." I shrugged, then looked into my cousin's eyes. "It's worth it. And it's not so horrible that every baby in the world is an only child, Jen."

"If men had babies, they would be," Loretta interjected spitefully.

Having given birth to two kidney stones, I am not sure I would disagree with her.

"Women have a much higher tolerance for pain," another woman stated to general nodding. Since I couldn't think of a single way to challenge this statement that didn't involve a contest in which we all had to experience pain, I didn't argue.

"I've had four babies, and my husband barely made it through each one. He almost passed out!" a woman boasted. Everyone laughed, even my cousin Jen.

No one seemed particularly mournful when I announced I needed to leave, but Jen walked me to the door, giving me a quick kiss on the cheek. "Thanks for coming, Bruce," she murmured, and I told her very sincerely that I was glad I did.

THE HORROR OF FENG SHUI

Another way a man might become more sensitive and in touch with himself is to expose himself to Eastern influences that have become very popular among nonmale segments of our population. One night my neighbor Tom called me while I was trying to decide between a roller polo match or a mud pull, flipping channels back and forth.

"You doing anything right now?" he wanted to know.

"No!" I responded eagerly. Tom has one of those new plasma televisions.

"I was wondering if you would come over and help me move some furniture."

"Oh. Well, actually, I'm pretty busy."

"It's feng shui," he said.

I thought about this. "I'd rather have Kentucky Fried Chicken," I told him.

"No, I mean . . . Can you just come over? Emily says we're supposed to hire some feng shui master, but I figure you and I could get this done ourselves, get all the elements of the universe in balance."

I was curious: Feng shui master? Elements of the universe? What was he talking about? "I'll pass," I said curiously.

"See, then I thought we could clean the junk out of my bass boat, get it ready for you to borrow."

"Okay, be right over," I decided.

Emily didn't seem very enthusiastic to see me. "This isn't going to work," she said, showing me in.

"I suppose we could go directly to the bass boat part," I speculated.

We gathered in the living room. "So tell him, Emily," Tom urged.

Emily sighed. "Feng shui is the ancient Chinese art of balancing the physical structures in our lives with the universe. A lot of it is just common sense, but it means rearranging the furniture, mirrors, things like that, to achieve harmony."

"That sounds pretty stupid," I responded open-mindedly.

"The first thing we did was starve ourselves," Tom interjected.

Emily sighed again. "What we did was eat a purifying diet for a few days, getting our bodies and minds receptive to the changes we'll be making. Each day, we wrote down our complaints in a journal. If you were a feng shui master, you'd read these now, to understand our mental state before we get started."

"Just hearing you talk, Emily, I think I have a real good idea of your mental state," I told her.

She looked at Tom. He cleared his throat. "Hey Bruce, so would you read these, or what?" He handed over his sheet of paper, and Emily did the same.

"Day one," I read from her paper. " 'Brown rice. Steamed vegetables.' " I peered at her. "This is how you felt?"

"It is what we ate," she snapped. "Read the rest of it."

"Okay. Um, 'My life is full of detail. It seems that more and more I have information, but less and less do I have truth. Is there meaning in all this mail crowding my mailbox, in all the sounds from the television and the radio? I am looking forward to simplifying my life. Today is the first day, I hope I will find more focus.' "

Tom and I exchanged bewildered glances. "You having some sort of trouble with the focus on your television?" I asked him.

Emily looked like she was rapidly losing patience, so I hurriedly read from Tom's sheet: " 'Day one. I am really, really hungry.' "

I beamed at them. "Good job, both of you!"

Emily just rolled her eyes.

"Now, Emily, day two," I announced. " 'Tossed salad with Chinese noodles. Rice and beans. Steamed broccoli.' " I nodded my approval. "Emily says, 'If purifying the body is the first step toward purifying my mind, I feel ready to take that step. I have a clearer sense of purpose, a resolve that we will find harmony if Tom and I work together. I feel I toil for material gain and have ignored my spiritual side. This is a new beginning.' Okay, very good! And now here is Tom's."

I paused. I had a feeling this wasn't going to go over very well with Emily. "Tom writes 'Ditto.' "

"Ditto?" Emily demanded.

"I meant, same as the day before," Tom explained.

"It was clear to me," I offered.

"You can't just say ditto every day!" Emily stormed.

"I didn't!" Tom protested.

I glanced down several days of "Ditto" and saw that he was indeed correct. " 'I am depressed today,' " I read from an entry at the bottom of the page, silencing them. " 'The Steelers lost.' " I glared at him. "You're a Steelers fan?"

"I grew up in Pittsburgh," he explained defensively.

"But you've lived here for ten years! When you move to a new town, you adopt the new home team! It's bad feng shui, otherwise!" I looked to Emily for support, but she seemed too irritated with Tom's team affiliation to be able even to speak about it.

We decided to move directly into the furniture-moving portion of the evening, and Emily's spirits improved somewhat. "Feng shui means wind and water," she told us helpfully.

That put Tom in mind of the joke about the guy who lived for a year on beans and water, but Emily refused to be drawn into our hilarity. I had a feeling Tom was going to need to rub a couple of feet after I left.

"The white tiger lives on the right side of the house, and the green dragon on the left," she announced.

"And do you *see* these animals, Emily?" I asked in a gentle voice.

She directed us to move a sofa because it was directly under a beam, which somehow put pressure on the family. She read from a feng shui manual, directing us to hang a small mirror to reflect bad spirits back out of the house. "How much did you pay for that book? Maybe I'll write a feng shui manual," I asked her.

"Do not store articles under the bed, it brings ill health," she read, ignoring me.

"Emily, if that were true, my daughters would have been sick every day of their lives."

"The bed itself should not be close to an open window during thunderstorms, as this will cause restlessness. . . ."

"And electrocution," I observed.

We put three coins in some red paper and buried them in a pot of soil in the prosperity corner, which I thought was pretty funny— I had trouble picturing a worse investment. Then we moved the dog bed out of the relationship corner, because having it there meant the dog was given equal status to the two of them in their marriage. "How can that be?" wondered Tom. "The dog never sleeps there, it sleeps with us!" Then we put a red scarf under their mattress, which supposedly would spice up their love life.

"Want to spice up your love life? Have the dog sleep somewhere else," I whispered to Tom when Emily was out of earshot.

Finally, we hung a photograph of Tom's mother-in-law in the family portion of the house, because, as Tom murmured to me, there apparently wasn't an old bat section.

The house now properly feng shuied, he and I went out to feng shui the bass boat. We cleaned out the future fish corner, and drank some beer from the happy ice chest.

BENDING OVER BACKWARD
FOR SARAH

Back at my own home, I assessed the placement of my furniture from a feng shui perspective. I might not have buried three coins in a pot of dirt, but I had several dollars worth of change lodged in my sofa cushions, and the dog wasn't in my relationship corner, but slept wherever there was a patch of sun on the carpet. I had taken care of my physical surroundings—now it was time to address my physical being.

I called Sarah and asked her if I could join her in her next yoga class, blinking when she said no.

"What? Why not?"

"Because it is the advanced class. It would be too hard," she informed me.

"Oh, advanced stretching? Advanced sitting cross-legged? I think I can manage."

She laughed and told me that one of the yoga studios she belonged to held both advanced classes and beginner classes, in separate rooms and at the same time. We arranged to meet in the lobby the next night.

"It's a date!" she said brightly, hanging up.

No, it wasn't a date, but her casual use of the word set loose a whole flood of thoughts in my head, all twisted and confused like a bunch of people in advanced yoga. After the class would be a perfect time to ask her out, if I wanted to. Did I want to?

Don't women hate it when male friends try to change the relationship to being something else? Yet I liked Sarah, she was fun and pretty and we had a lot in common. Why shouldn't we go out? But what if she said no? Why isn't there someplace on the Internet where you can look up stuff like this?

When Sarah walked through the front doors my heart began beating furiously, which was ridiculous because I saw her nearly every day! I was mute as she signed me up for the class, and she regarded me curiously.

"You okay?"

"I'm yes," I responded for some reason.

She laughed. "Don't worry, you'll be fine. Head on in there, and I'll meet you out here afterward."

I filed into the back of the beginner yoga room and took my position on one of the mats, noting that I was one of only a couple of men out of the dozen or so students.

Yoga, as it turns out, is sort of like playing Twister, only every position into which you thrust yourself has a name. For example, standing with your hips in the air, your feet apart, your hands on the floor, and your shoulders dislocated is something like Downward Stabbing Chicken. Rotate your hips and stretch your back until your vertebrae pop like firecrackers, and it's called Warrior Needing Orthopedist. I was reminded of when I was young and I would remove the heads from my sister's dolls and take the plastic legs and stick them in the arm sockets: Decapitated Barbie.

I was actually pretty good at yoga, with the instructor calling out appreciative comments like, "Mr. Cameron, please stop falling on the other students!" and "Who is making that whimpering sound?" By the end of the session, I lay in the Collapsed Dog position, exhausted but glad that I had gone through the whole ordeal. Flexibility is one of the three important elements of long-term health, the other two being naps and rest.

Next came meditation. Each of us sat on our mats, with our legs crossed and our fingers held in what is called the "Weird" position. I was reminded of my first day of kindergarten, and started to tell a hilarious story about how I ate too much paste and had to have my stomach pumped, when the instructor interrupted me and asked me to please stop talking—apparently Meditation Time is the same as No Sense of Humor Time. None of the other students said anything, though I am sure they are probably to this day wondering how the story turned out.

The instructor told us to concentrate on our breathing. "Always exhale," she said. I put this in the "well duh" category and felt that we were ready for maybe a little more advanced instruction, like "Don't eat the paste," ha ha.

"Go to a peaceful place, by the water," she suggested. "Ask yourself, how does it smell? What do you hear?"

I took a deep sniff. It smelled like people's sweaty feet. Mostly what I could hear was everybody's breathing. Some of the students were acting like raspy breathing was going to get them an "A" in the class.

"Now, softly, your own personal chant," the instructor told us. Everyone immediately began to drone, making sounds like "Wullllllllll" and "Weeeeeeeee." I didn't have a personal chant, so it took me a little while to come up with one.

"Weeeeeee

"Wulllllllllll

"Weeeeee

"Wullllllllll

"Rock you"

"Mr. Cameron, please stop whatever it is you are doing," I was instructed.

We then lay on our backs, the lights were turned low, and we were advised to think of a river, moving down stream, slower and slower, wider and deeper. "Let your thoughts float where they will, along the surface of the water," I was told, so I decided I would probably use a Mepps treble hook and cast along the banks.

"Don't think about your bills, about your job . . . just stay with the river," she intoned.

I couldn't believe that if she wanted us to not think about something, she would mention it. Do you know how hard it is to not think of something once someone has brought it up?

"Mr. Cameron, please stop talking during meditation," she remonstrated gently.

Eventually I was able to stop thinking about my debts and my insurance premiums and my deadlines, things the instructor called monkey thoughts, as if you'll ever see a chimpanzee with a credit card, and just float along, though I never could manage to see with my third eye. Apparently we were doing cyclops meditation, ha ha. Or triclops.

"Mr. Cameron, please? We need total silence."

I closed my eyes and worked on thinking about absolutely nothing. It wasn't as difficult as I imagined it might be.

After the class, as a joke, several of my classmates came up to me and claimed that I had snored. They also asked if I would be coming back to any more classes, which I found rather flattering. "The only other night I can do it is on Tuesdays, you're not going to start on Tuesdays, are you?" I was asked by one woman.

Sarah was already out front, waiting for me. "How was it?" she inquired eagerly.

"Now I know how Gumby feels."

She laughed, putting her arm through mine. "You had a really good instructor for the first time. Very gentle."

"Gentle? She tried to get me to break my own hip."

We stopped at Sarah's car. "Once you get to know your body better, you'll find you really enjoy yoga," she suggested.

"I already know my body. I sleep with it every night!"

We stood there a moment, a lull in the conversation moving in like the fog. It would be a perfect time to ask her out. *Want to go out to dinner with me? Want to go grab a bite? How about we go grab dinner? A bite of dinner. What's say you and I grab a dinner? We should go somewhere, I'd like to grab you.*

Sarah sighed. "Well. . . ."

And I said . . . nothing. Well, not nothing. "See you tomorrow," is what I said, turning and walking away fast, like fleeing the scene of a crime. I got in my car and started the motor, but waited until I saw Sarah drive out of the parking lot before I departed.

THE MORE SPIRITUAL ME

As a Changed Man, fully in touch with his feelings and with an appreciation of life enhanced by Eastern thought, I now realize that everything I possess has its own place in the universe. For example, my son's bicycle apparently belongs in my garage, blocking my car. Inanimate objects have feelings, which is why my socks have legally separated, and my roof weeps every time it rains. Many of the things I buy find they would rather be in the part of the universe known as my daughter's apartment, and the dollars in my savings account seem bent on running away from home.

My body and mind also belong in the universe, because, well, they aren't sure what alternatives might be available. I'm constantly in touch with myself:

BRUCE:

Self, you there?

SELF:

Yep!

BRUCE:

Okay, just wanted to make sure.

SELF:

Stay in touch!

I am at peace, secure in the knowledge that because of feng shui, I can borrow Tom's boat next weekend.

If you want to remodel your man to make him more sensitive, spiritual, and in touch with himself, you'll have to figure out a way to get him to agree to expose himself to the influences of different foreign cultures, like the Buddhists of ancient Tibet or the cab drivers of New York. Gradually he'll grow increasingly accepting, especially if you agree to go out for margaritas after the yoga class.

In time, you'll hear him make such statements as, "I think it would be good feng shui if we could sign up for more sports channels on cable." At that moment, you can take pride in the fact that you did it: You changed your man.

17.

— — —

BIRTH OF A CHANGED MAN

A Newborn Perspective

I don't know what I expected, once I declared to the world that I was a Changed Man, though universal adoration would have been nice. I know that awesome social attributes are not always immediately evident to some people, but once you point them out, you'd think everyone would be able to remember you have them. I guess I pictured having conversations like this:

ME:

I'm a Changed Man.

EVERYONE:

We adore you!

Instead, I found myself having a conversation with my neighbor Tom about the bug zapper he owned when he lived in Pittsburgh.

A bug zapper is a device that looks like a large streetlight but is actually a place where insects willingly go to be electrocuted. I'm pretty sick of hearing about the stupid thing, but we were visiting our friend Hurly, and the disgusted expression on Hurly's face made another retelling worth suffering through.

It was a perfect evening. We were sitting on Hurly's back deck, eating the watermelon his wife had kindly provided, the watermelon seeds flying "like bugs falling from a backyard bug zapper," as Tom put it, which gives you a sense of Tom's single-mindedness about the discussion. Tom was only occasionally successful in spitting past the deck railing, but Hurly was too polite to ask his neighbor to quit dribbling seeds all over the place.

Watching this little drama unfold before me, I was struck by three great truths—a simultaneous flash of insights hitting me in the sort of multidimensional cognitive thinking at which men are so expert.

The ability to hold three separate concepts together in our minds is the reason why men are so much better than women at making critical decisions in times of great importance, like during video games.

GREAT TRUTH # 1: Though arguably males of the same species, Tom, Hurly, and I could not have been more diverse. It was as if we were each fierce, proud jungle cats, of similar lineage but as different as a puma, cougar, and mountain lion.* So some of my remodeling tips, while they worked for me, might not be as effective on someone less sophisticated.

GREAT TRUTH # 2: Despite our differences, none of us would ever put any pressure on the other to change, though I suppose Hurly would have been a little happier with less watermelon juice on his back deck.

---

*When I pointed this out to Hurly, he frowned and informed me that a puma, cougar, and mountain lion are all the same species. Which okay might be true, but not everyone knows that, so I still think it is a valid comparison.

GREAT TRUTH # 3: I forgot the third Great Truth, but I remember it was pretty impressive.

"So what you do, is, you put a coffee can under the zapper, and on a good night you can fill it up," Tom was saying.

"With . . . dead bugs?" Hurly asked.

"Fried. Fried dead bugs," Tom clarified.

"A coffee can full of fried, dead bugs," Hurly repeated. He gave me an imploring look, but all I could do was shrug—I'd never lived in Pittsburgh.

No amount of remodeling was going to turn Hurly into a man like Tom unless it involved brain damage, but maybe that was a good thing. Maybe the world needs men like Tom to spit watermelon seeds and men like Hurly to clean them up. As much as their wives probably wished both men could be more like me, Emily obviously loved Tom—she bought him a new outboard motor for Christmas—and Juliet could never walk past Hurly without reaching out to touch him on the shoulder or on the back of the neck.

"But what could you possibly want with a can full of burned-up insects?" Hurly pressed.

"What do you mean?" Tom replied, baffled.

Hurly didn't understand that the coffee can piled high with zapped bugs was just a way of keeping score, of saying, "I'm a real man, I killed a whole bunch of flying insects!" And Tom couldn't begin to comprehend that to a man like Hurly, sitting on a patio in Pittsburgh, bathed in the blue light from the zapper, listening as the intoxicated insects danced too close and burned in an electric flash before falling with an audible plink into a coffee can was something almost exactly the opposite of fun.

They were different men, because they were motivated by different things. My remodeling techniques would work on any man, but with varying success depending on their individual needs, wants, and desires.

That's it, the one I forgot!

GREAT TRUTH # 3: The most effective way to remodel a man is to motivate him through love, though it's probably more fun to use trickery and manipulation.

A MOTIVATING STORY

One weekday afternoon I was deeply focused on a particularly difficult passage in a piece I was writing when the telephone rang, startling me awake.

"Hello?"

"It's Jen."

"Who?"

"Your cousin Jen."

"Jen! How are you? How are things in the good old fetal development department?"

"Well, that's why I'm calling. Can you come over? It's starting."

"Sorry?"

"My labor is starting."

I gripped the phone. "What? No! It can't be starting! You're not due until the Super Bowl . . . We're barely into the playoffs!"

"I know. It looks like it is going to be early. Can you . . . could you come over?"

Her plaintive voice stopped me. Clearly, she needed reassurance, a sense that I, her favorite cousin, would be there for her in her time of need. "Where the hell is your husband?" I barked.

"Glenn's in London."

"London? London, England?"

"Actually, he's already on a plane back, but he won't be here for several more hours," she explained.

"Well, that won't do at all!" I observed bitterly. "Don't you think that's a little self-centered of him, to be flying around all over the world when his wife was so far along? I mean, I have a lot of stuff going on and now I suppose I just have to drop everything, which I am willing to do without complaint, but I do think he sort of is missing the point of what is important, here."

"Ahh . . ." she replied, her voice distant.

"Jen? What's the matter?" I asked, in what I now realize was one of the ten dumbest questions ever asked in the history of mankind. A human being was trying to climb out of her body, and I wanted to know what was the matter?

"A contraction," she murmured.

"A what? Okay! Okay! Don't panic. Jen, do not panic." I raced out of the room, then decided to return when the phone cord snapped taut. "You are going to be fine! Everything's under control!" I shouted calmly. "We have nothing to fear but fear itself!"

"Oh!" she said sharply.

"What happened? Did the baby just get born?"

"My water broke."

This seemed totally unfair. I took a deep breath. "Jen, I want you to call nine-one-one. I'm coming over, but this seems to be happening awfully fast. Call an ambulance, okay?"

"Okay," she agreed weakly.

I hung up. "Oh my God! Oh my God!"

It is at times like these when it is good to be a man. Eons of evolution have given us the ability to turn threat into opportunity. As I ran for the car, the adrenaline in my system sharpening my senses, I saw the cat as if she were in slow motion as she lay sleeping in the corner. I bounded gracefully down the stairs, leaping over a stack of folded laundry with all the athletic precision of an Olympic runner knocking over hurdles. My stupid dog, responding to the burst of energy, began barking maniacally, but I remained focused. In the garage, I perceived with absolute clarity that I had forgotten the car keys, so I sprinted back inside, tripping over my canine and

262 | HOW TO REMODEL A MAN

knocking myself flat. He jumped on me, trying to lick my face. Mittens came to the top of the stairs and regarded us both with disgust.

Up the stairs. Mittens's eyes widened, and she bolted away. Find my pants. Fish the keys out of the pocket. Back down the stairs. Dodge the dog, who was leaping and barking in frenzied joy. Jump in the car. Key in. Garage door up. Start car, put it in reverse.

Pause.

Something didn't seem right. I mentally reviewed what had just happened, and decided that while I was digging in my jeans for the car keys, it would have been a good time to put on some pants.

Back inside. My dog seized the pants in his teeth, shaking his head from side to side as I tried to put them on. "No! Bad dog! Idiot! Would you stop? Jen is having a baby!" I scolded. I promised him that if he would just behave, I would take him to visit the new mother, like those hospital-trained dogs utilized to calm sick patients. This was patently a lie; my dog is so hyper, his presence in the hospital would be about as calming as the running of the bulls.

This lie seem to get to my pet, who has always been fond of Jen. He reluctantly released the pant leg. I charged back down the stairs, got in the car, and drove through the streets like a teenager late for curfew.

The ambulance was already there, and Jen was on the stretcher, being wheeled outside, her pretty face pale. She'd taken the time to brush her hair, and for some reason this nearly broke my heart, that she had to get ready to go to the hospital, all by herself. I knew from her expression that she was frightened, and resolved that I would show her a steady reassurance. "Bruce. My water broke," she whispered sadly.

"I know, you told me. It's okay, we'll fix it."

"Can you ride with me to the hospital?"

"Yes! Of course!" I jumped into the back of the ambulance, then got back out so that they could load the stretcher.

The ride in was awful, with gasping and teeth-gnashing and panting—and Jen was doing even worse. Twice during the short trip she went white-lipped, slipping into moments of sheer agony.

And whom did we run into at the front doors? Nurse Satan from Lamaze class. I could only hope she wouldn't remember me.

"Welcome back, Mr. Cameron," she greeted evenly.

"Okay, she's having the baby. Her water is broken. Possible cervical dilation. We need to go right into massive surgery," I stated professionally.

The nurse was absently checking pulse and things like that, as if we had all the time in the world. She asked a bunch of irrelevant questions, like how far apart were the contractions—plainly, this woman had no head for emergency work. "You need to steady your breathing, you keep panting like that you're going to pass out," the nurse stated at one point.

"I'm not panting," I snapped irritably.

We were led into the birthing room. Everyone was in a state of unflustered tranquility, which I didn't think was helping matters much at all. Jen was having a baby. I wanted to see warning lights and people running around in unisex uniforms while a loudspeaker broadcast, "Six minutes to baby. All systems go."

Only, as it turned out, we were nowhere near six minutes to baby. I remembered my training and started to help Jen breathe, and after a while it seemed to make some sort of difference, because I no longer felt like throwing up.

Jen had elected to have natural childbirth, which astounded me. "No painkillers?" I demanded. "How can that be considered natural?"

I'd been through this before, of course. I have three children, and all of them were born. But the obstetrician who delivered my offspring had a pretty aggressive attitude toward medication, and by this point in the process with my own three kids I'd already been given a lot of Valium.

I talked to Glenn, Jen's husband, as he switched planes at JFK, and was comforted that at least he was in a state of hysteria. I felt that this was the wrong time to point out the fact that he shouldn't have been off running around Europe with his wife so pregnant, but I did it anyway, leading to a rather heated debate over whether or not England is in Europe or is different because it is part of the British Isles. Arguing vehemently about unimportant issues is the sort of thing that men do to relieve stress, so when I realized why he was focused so rabidly on such an irrelevancy, I sympathetically told him that I understood his tension, and not to worry, everything was okay and I wouldn't hold it against him for being so wrong in his geography.

Jen was experiencing back labor, which meant that with every contraction, I needed to push down on her lower back to help relieve the pain. Ironically, the doctors told her she wasn't allowed to do any pushing herself, at least not yet.

The birthing room was darkly lit, and a CD Jen had selected played a steady selection of nature sounds—babbling brooks and trickling waters—which was supposed to be relaxing but which made me need to use the bathroom. For long stretches of time I was alone with Jen, pushing on her back when she needed it, standing around rather worthlessly when she didn't. When the nurse came in, I was always ready with my updated report, which usually could be distilled down to the observation that "The baby is coming out."

"It will be some time yet," I was always told. I hardly took comfort in this prediction—these were the same people who missed Jen's due date by more than three weeks.

"These people aren't paying any attention to me," I seethed to Sarah when I finally reached her with my cell phone.

"They probably think Jen has a higher priority," she agreed sympathetically.

She said she would of course come pick me up when it was all over, no matter what time of day or night. We hung up so I could get back to Jen for the next contraction. "It's time," I announced to the nursing station as I hurried past.

Finally everyone seemed to take my medical diagnosis seriously. They assembled to catch the baby, while I sat up by Jen's head and answered the same question over and over.

"Are you sure you're not going to pass out?"

"Yes, of course I'm sure."

"Are you sure you're not going to pass out?"

"Yes, of course I'm sure."

And I didn't pass out, though when the baby emerged, the room went dark and I wound up flat on my back with a nurse patting my cheek. Jen had given birth to a little girl who seemed even more disoriented than I, glancing around the room at all these masked strangers. They promptly gave her an Apgar quiz, sort of an SAT for babies. She passed with good enough grades to get into Harvard. She was handed over to her mother, and for a minute, everyone seemed pretty pleased with the job I had done.

But then things changed.

The doctor became alarmed, and Jen's color went to a frightening white. She was bleeding too much, and suddenly the baby was thrust into my arms while they rushed Jen out of the room to surgery.

You want to remodel a man? Hand him a little girl less than an hour old and leave it to him to explain to her what's going on. I snuggled her to my chest, her blankets still warm from the heater, and told her that in the whole, grand world there was no person more important than she was at that moment. I even sang to her a little, but her expression was not very encouraging so I gave it up. Apparently she was a little young for Lynyrd Skynyrd.

I was reminded of the birth of my first child. Before my daughter came along, my main goal in life was to make enough money to buy a Porsche. Then I was given a little bundle in a hospital room just like this one, and my priorities rearranged themselves like an amateur dance troupe out of position when the curtain goes up. For many years, my children were the single strongest source of joy in my life, and then they became teenagers and made me want to kill myself.*

I don't know how long I spent in that magical place, the room dim and the background sounds of a waterfall filling the air, before Glenn burst into the room. He was dressed in surgical garb, having been intercepted as he charged into the hospital and directed to Jen's side.

"She's okay," Glenn told me. "It was just something up . . . You know, up there, inside her reproductive organs."

We shared a panicky expression, terrified that circumstances might force us to talk about the inner workings of a woman's body.

"They fixed it. She just needed some stitches. She's fine now."

I told him how relieved I was, but he was looking at the bundle in my arms. "Is that . . . her?" he finally asked. As if I would be sitting in the maternity wing of the hospital with someone else's baby.

"Here. It's your new daughter," I replied, gently handing over the little girl.

He caught his breath as he gathered her up. I watched the transformation take him—he'd flown all night, and the fatigue was etched deeply into his eyes, but now, holding his newborn child, his whole body came alive.

He looked at me. "I need to get a different job," he whispered. "I can't travel this much anymore."

"I know," I agreed.

"She's beautiful."

"She sure is," I replied. "I named her 'Bruceina.' "

"Oh. Uh . . ." He seemed touched beyond words.

We admired her for a little while longer, and then it occurred to

---

* *8 Simple Rules for Dating My Teenage Daughter,* Cameron, Workman Publishing, May 2001.

me that my presence was no longer required. Jen and Glenn had remodeled from being a couple to being a family, and they didn't need me around anymore. I told him I would be leaving, and he thanked me for all I had done. "Actually, it was Jen who did all the work," I informed him. I phoned Sarah, then went to clean myself up a little.

On the way out of the hospital, the sunset a glorious, grand-finale orange, I saw a woman coming toward me. For a moment, we were alone in the tiny glass room between the outer pair of doors and the inner pair, a place for the heated inside air to mingle with the wintry air from the outside and get used to each other. I'm afraid I stared, because I recognized who it was: Susie, from Teen Town.

A lot of years had passed since junior high school, but her eyes were still exactly the same. She always had this mischievous glint to them, like there was some sort of practical joke going on, something only she knew about. It had been that laughing look in her eyes that captivated me when I was a teen—a hundred years could go by, and I would still know who she was. I stopped dead, but she didn't pause, though she did glance curiously at me as I stood there with my mouth open. I didn't see any recognition in her eyes as they briefly assessed me. And then the inner doors spread open in pneumatic greeting and she passed through them and into the hospital. They remained that way, inviting me to follow her in, but I stayed rooted to the spot until they eased shut with a sigh that sounded like gentle recrimination.

And the whole time, I never said a word.

PUNCH LIST

Sarah showed up a few minutes later. I jumped in her car. "Well, I did it!" I told her.

For some reason women always want to know how much the baby weighed, but men don't see the relevance. I hadn't paid attention to this detail, so I just guessed.

"Thirty pounds?" Sarah demanded, horrified.

"Did I say pounds? I meant ounces."

"Only thirty ounces?" she challenged. "It was a full-term pregnancy."

"No it wasn't, this was supposed to interrupt the Super Bowl."

"Find out for me tomorrow, I want to know."

"Oh fine," I grumbled.

We drove for a minute in silence. I looked at her, my eyes drawn to her profile, which was so much prettier now that Doug was in Cleveland.

She glanced at me. "What?" she wanted to know.

At that moment my mind flashed back to Susie from Teen Town, for some reason. My mouth opened.

"Bruce?" Sarah asked curiously.

"You want to maybe go get a bite to eat?" I blurted.

"Sure," she said casually.

I frowned. Clearly, she didn't understand.

"I mean like a date. It would be a date, you and me, out to dinner."

She laughed. "I know."

"Okay then," I said grimly.

"Okay."

She glanced my way, and we smiled at each other. This one, I reflected, was definitely worth remodeling myself for.